W9-BKI-632

STONY CREEK LIBRARY
1350 GREENFIELD PIKE
NOBLESVILLE, IN 46060

Richard Peck

A Spellbinding Storyteller

Kimberly Campbell

Enslow Publishers, Inc.
40 Industrial Road
Box 398
Berkeley Heights, NJ 07922
USA
http://www.enslow.com

Copyright © 2008 by Kimberly Campbell

All rights reserved.

No part of this book may be reproduced by any means without the written permission of the publisher.

Library of Congress Cataloging-in-Publication Data

Campbell, Kimberly, 1971–
    Richard Peck : a spellbinding storyteller / by Kimberly Campbell.
       p. cm. — (Authors teens love)
    Includes bibliographical references and index.
    ISBN-13: 978-0-7660-2723-7
    ISBN-10: 0-7660-2723-6
    1. Peck, Richard, 1934–   —Juvenile literature. 2. Authors,
American—20th century—Biography—Juvenile literature. 3. Young adult
fiction—Authorship—Juvenile literature. I. Title.
    PS3566.E2526Z63 2007
    813'.54—dc22

                                2006034069

Printed in the United States of America

102011 The HF Group, North Manchester, IN

10 9 8 7 6 5 4 3 2

To Our Readers: We have done our best to make sure all Internet Addresses in this book were active and appropriate when we went to press. However, the author and publisher have no control over and assume no liability for the material available on those Internet sites or on other Web sites they may link to. Any comments or suggestions can be sent by e-mail to comments@enslow.com or to the address on the back cover.

Cover Illustration: Mark A. Hicks (background); Richard Peck (foreground).

Photos and Illustrations: All images courtesy of Richard Peck.

38888000189781

CONTENTS

CHAPTER 1

BURNING BRIDGES

On May 24, 1971, Richard Peck quit his teaching job at a junior high school to become an author. That same day, at the ripe old age of thirty-seven, he wrote his first line of fiction. Quitting his job to chase a dream was the catalyst that launched his writing career. Leaving a steady paycheck behind was a risky decision, but Peck had the nerve to do it. At a writing workshop years later he admits, "You must write by the light of the bridges burning behind you."[1] Burning the bridge to his immediate past—that of English teacher—was his glorious and fearful beginning act. Here is that first line of fiction, the opening line of *Don't Look and It Won't Hurt*:

> Out at the city limits, there's this sign that says; WELCOME TO CLAYPITTS, PEARL OF THE PRAIRIE, and if you'd believe that you'd believe anything.[2]

That first jobless evening, Peck recalls grasping the term "generation gap." He wondered where his readers came from, with nearly half of them a product of imperfect families: divorced parents, stepparents, working parents, and some who had experienced loss. Peck certainly felt the changing of the social tide and the erosion of the family unit, so he focused his stories primarily around traditional family life.

Peck had insecure moments about his decision to become a writer. In retrospect, he says, "I went home to write or die."[3] Still, he wondered if he could write even *one* novel. For the next four months, he worked on that novel. When he set out to sell it, he hand carried the manuscript to George Nicholson, a juvenile editor for Holt, Rinehart and Winston (now Henry Holt). Nicholson called him the following morning and told Peck to go ahead and begin a second novel.[4]

With his first book, *Don't Look and It Won't Hurt*, accepted for publication literally overnight, he was officially published in 1972. Selling a book in just twenty-four hours is an exceptional feat in the world of publishing, but Peck had done it.

Ironically, his debut novel was not about his students, but about his friends Dr. and Mrs. Richard Hughes, who operated a home for unwed mothers in Evanston, Illinois. Peck had asked the Hughes about the girls at this home, and from these discussions, he gleaned a scant outline.[5] *Don't Look and It Won't Hurt* (Holt, Rinehart and

Winston, 1972) was later made into the 1992 movie *Gas Food Lodging*.

Peck soon received a bushel of letters from his newfound readership, which caused him to hit the road, calling on schools and libraries. He began sharing ideas and reflections on his writing process with youngsters all over the country. But mostly he listened to the young voices, and he brooded over what he heard. Visiting these schools confirmed Peck's beliefs about his students' lives: most were from fragmented families—typically with "missing" fathers—or suffering from painful dysfunctional relationships.

This disturbing reality left Peck more determined to write stories that touched the lives of teens. He wanted to provide them with a recognizable, common father. The desire to deal with the topic of teens living without their father (in the home) inspired him to write his second novel, *Father Figure*. The book is about a seventeen-year-old boy's efforts to compensate for his absent father. Peck says, "Confronting a generation of boys without fathers when I couldn't fathom growing up without my own may have been the novel's real inspiration. On the day I finished it, my father died, and at forty-three I was as lost as I would have been at any moment before."[6]

Throughout his boyhood, Peck was surrounded by eccentric and lively relatives, including his father, who drove around town on a Harley-Davidson motorcycle wearing overalls. His father managed a Phillips 66 gas station, where all the town codgers would gather and gossip. From his father, Peck says, "I learned nostalgia as an art form."[7]

By mastering the art of eavesdropping as a child, Peck developed an uncanny connection to—and affinity for—the past. He has a knack for meshing truth and imagination. He gave life to the fictional Grandma Dowdel in *A Year Down Yonder*, and other "old," whimsical characters who play major roles in most of his novels. Peck says of these unusual older folks who star in his books, "They provide wisdom and seasoning won only through long lifetimes . . . the battered old survivors who stalk through my pages embody the truth upon which all fiction turns: that in the long run, you will be held responsible for the consequences of your actions."[8]

Peck carried the voices of his past inside his head, and it was not until later that they began to appear as fictional characters in his novels. "I came to writing with an entire crew of seasoned elders on my side," he says.[9] Surrounded as a child by colorful (and even sometimes kooky or rogue) relatives and townsfolk, his memory was saturated with rich and lovable people. Knowing these souls served him well when he decided to portray their unique personalities in his stories.

Another special spot where young Peck observed the intricacies of humanity, setting, and scenery was his grandparents' farm. He spent a lot of time at Walnut Grove Farm, listening to his kinfolks' retellings of their pasts. The voices of this Victorian era later brought the personality and

Richard Peck in May 2005. As an author, Peck has a knack for meshing truth with imagination.

voice of Blossom Culp to life.[10] Blossom is a teenage girl growing up in the 1910s (a character in Peck's book series) who has psychic powers.

Peck grew up in a loving home with support from a large, extended family. His mother first cultivated his interest in learning because she read to him a lot. From a child-sized, wooden table along their kitchen wall, Peck would listen to his mother as she stood at the sink teaching him spelling and grammar. He was taught how to write thank-you notes, and did so for every gift he received. This foundation of a good vocabulary is perhaps one reason why he advises anyone who wants to be a writer to be a reader first. Peck believes that you should read a thousand books before trying to write one.

It was the influence of school—that place where teachers, students, puberty, peer influences, and rites of passages collide—where Peck "first became aware of the special problems of adolescents and identified his potential readers: the quiet, independent-minded students who could be won over to reading. This experience with teenagers growing up in rootless suburbia was to profoundly affect Peck's later young adult novels."[11]

Peck's students have unquestionably left their mark on him as a writer. He wrote a poem about them called "A Teenager's Prayer":

Oh, Supreme Being, and I don't mean me:
Give me the vision to see my parents as human beings
because if they aren't, what does that make me?
Give me vocabulary because the more I say you know,
the less anyone does.
Give me freedom from television because I'm beginning
to distrust its happy endings.
Give me sex education to correct what I first heard
from thirteen-year-olds.
Give me homework to keep me from flunking Free Time.
Give me a map of the world so I may see that this town
and I are not the center of it.
Give me the knowledge that conformity is the enemy of
friendship.
Give me the understanding that nobody grows up in a
group,
so that I may find my own way.
Give me limits so that I will know I'm loved.
And give me nothing I haven't earned so that this
adolescence
will not last forever.
                                        Amen[12]

His students were the reason he became a writer. Peck's decision—to leave the "adult" world and pursue a writing career in children's literature—is one that many people are too scared to try. But speaking about that first burned bridge (quitting his old teaching job), he admits, "Teaching is a job you never really quit. You just go on and on trying to turn life into lesson plans." So it is Peck's insightful quote, "You must write by the light of the bridges burning behind you," that best describes his quest to become an author.

Although Peck has burned a few bridges in order to heed the call of writing and to extract the humorous and poignant stories within him, he has also *built* bridges as well—to the younger generation through his expressive writing, school visits, and literacy efforts. When asked by one of his readers about the pressure of writing a book, Peck says, "Very few people would choose to live in this kind of isolation, and do work this speculative, but then writers aren't most people."[13]

His was a glorious, fearful beginning, one born on faith that would eventually lead him down a successful path where dreams of London, the New York literary scene, a captivating body of work and, eventually, the Newbery Medal were well within this Midwestern farm boy's grasp.

CHAPTER 2

FARMING THE FOLKS

Whether Richard knew it or not then, he was being groomed at an early age to be a reader. His mother, Virginia Gray, is due much of the credit. She was a key mentor for him. Richard sat upon his mother's knee, and she read to him before he could read himself. It was there upon her lap where he got his beginning. "She wasn't trying to make me a published writer. She was trying to make me a successful first-grader."[1] Speaking about the early learning experience he says, "The minute she opened the door to the alternative universe of stories, of fiction, I saw more interesting lives than mine, and I still do."[2]

Born on April 5, 1934, in Decatur, Illinois, he was reared in a white frame house next to Fairview Park. He grew up in small-town America in the heart of the Midwest. As a boy, he spent time at a child-sized table and chair along the kitchen wall, where his mother recited phrases as Richard practiced writing. She taught him how to write his ABCs. As she stood by the sink, she called out letters of the alphabet and spelled words for him. He wrote a thank-you letter for every gift he received from his grandparents. With this early training, Richard's mother gave him a head start on mastering punctuation and the written word, and perhaps a lesson or two on politeness and good manners.

Because of his mother's devotion to reading to him, he was enticed into the mesmerizing art of language. "She intoxicated me with words," Peck recalled. He fell in love with the lives of characters in books. "Would I rather have been belly-flopping on a Flexible Flyer down the steepest hill in Fairview Park?" "Maybe," he admits in retrospect. But he was glad for the chance to get ahead of the pack in his classes.[3] His mother read folktales by the Brothers Grimm, the wanderlust stories of Richard Halliburton, and the *National Geographic* magazines that arrived monthly at their home. In his usual blend of eloquence, wit, and sarcasm, Richard Peck now lovingly boasts about his mother's literary guidance when he was a tot. "She had no intention of sending an ignoramus to first grade!"[4]

But nobody is perfect. In fact, growing up, Richard had a habit. By his own admission, Peck was a born eavesdropper. He listened in on townsfolk, family, and friends. Not only did he get an earful, but he also gained an insider's view of his hometown's scenery—people, places, peculiar behaviors, and even the occasional wild rumor.

In 1939, near the time that Richard started kindergarten at Dennis Grade School, Adolf Hitler's army invaded Poland. Thus, wartime chatter became second nature to the adults in Richard's world. It was a topic discussed at home and around town. Grown-ups often disagreed, and lively arguments ensued. From these spats, Richard learned "viewpoint." For a writer of fiction, viewpoint is defined as the perspective from which a story is told; the narrator's position in relation to the story. Talk of soldiers, foreign words, and faraway places opened Richard's mind to the fact that exciting things were happening outside Decatur's city limits.[5]

Richard also observed his father, Wayne M. Peck, who zoomed down the streets of town on a Harley-Davidson motorcycle. His father ran a Phillips 66 gas station, and he usually wore overalls. In that gas station, twelve-year-old boys rolled their newspapers, worked hard on their macho vocabulary and hoped to be believed. At the filling station he was also privy to the conversations and tall tales of older men—old truckers, farmers, and railroaders. It was a club of sorts, a cast of elderly fellows. From these dueling generations of men and boys, Richard learned vocabulary beyond his years.[6]

By far the most free-spirited and quirky relative he had was his great-uncle Miles, an eighty-something-year-old carpenter. He had married several times, but apparently "not seriously." He drove a Model A Ford around town. Richard learned more than foulmouthed language from this gossiping troublemaker. He also learned local history. Peck later used his uncle as a major character in *The Ghost Belonged to Me* (Viking, 1975).[7]

Somewhere along the way, in the seemingly quiet streets of Decatur, Richard became an historian. He stockpiled a mountain of humorous, charming, and oftentimes downright wild accounts of the past, and the people he had known. He later drew from childhood experiences—time spent with parents, grandparents, extended family, friends, and other citizens of Decatur. This rural backdrop later heavily influenced his books, poems, and stories.

Peck is proud of his hometown and the region he hails from. These days he asks rhetorically, "Imagine wanting to hide it?" Peck does not necessarily come from a long line of storytellers. He says, "But it was a family with secrets. And that was more interesting. All families have secrets."[8]

Richard's extended family was a steady, assuring presence, especially his aunts. They all played an important role in his upbringing. Along the way, he gained a younger sister, Cheryl, when he was in third grade. In his youth, Richard was sufficiently outnumbered by women. His Aunt Rozella, who had lived with them for the first fifteen years of Richard's life, told him many a

STONY CREEK LIBRARY
1350 GREENFIELD PIKE
NOBLESVILLE, IN 46060

tale. His grandmother, Flossie Mae Gray, and her four sisters, Pearl, Mura, Maude, and Ozena, lived at the Walnut Grove farm. Richard heard many lively stories from them about the nineteenth century. The old-fashioned phrases, expressions, and mannerisms his great-aunts used brought the voice of Blossom Culp to life in his fifth book, *The Ghost Belonged to Me*.[9] In Blossom, there is more than a hint of one of Twain's all-time beloved characters, Huckleberry Finn.[10]

Richard discovered a love for Mark Twain's books while growing up and deemed him the greatest writer of the Midwest. Even now, Peck pays homage to Mark Twain's work in his own books to try to thank him. Speaking about Twain today he says, "All American stories flow from one." Peck keeps a copy of *The Adventures of Huckleberry Finn* on his writing desk in his New York apartment.[11]

As a boy, Peck spent time between his home in Decatur and his grandparents' farm—the Walnut Grove Farm. The farm was once run by his great-grandfather, William Gray, who was an immigrant from Ireland. His great-grandfather had come to own the land in 1852, and it was passed down to his son John, who farmed it until 1964.

In its heyday, the farm thrived, and young Richard enjoyed good times there. He still has fond memories of it. The farm served as the setting for his one and only picture book, *Monster Night at Grandma's House* (Viking, 1977). At Grandma's old house, daytime is fun and nighttime is scary.

It stars a young boy named Toby, who, lying alone upstairs in bed late at night, believes some "thing" is standing in his room.

> Then he heard the night bugs hitting the window screen. The longer he listened, the more those bugs sounded like fingers. Some were little tapping fingers. Some were big poking fingers. And some were scratching fingers that didn't sound a bit like bugs.

> On this worst night of all, that floorboard creaked. Toby knew there were no such things as monsters. Besides, he was brave for his age. He wanted to sit right up in bed and say, "WHO'S THERE AND WHAT DO YOU WANT?"[12]

As a kid, Richard had another uncommon trait. He never missed a homework assignment. He says later, "I did homework out of fear, not goodness. From junior high on, I thought that the only safe way to a scholarship was a string of A's on the report card." In comparison to most teens, young Richard never rebelled and followed all the proper rules. He obeyed his teachers without fail. He was hardworking, running a paper route after school with his buddy. By doing so, he learned responsibility.

One summer, sixteen-year-old Richard took a trip to New York City to visit a relative. Just to pay his way there he remembers, "I raked yards and shoveled snow for a chair car ticket on the Pennsylvania Railroad." He explored the underground world of the subway system and traveled as far as Coney Island. Richard knew someday he would return to New York City. The trip deeply rooted the idea in his brain that there was something magical and magnetic there.[13]

By the time he reached Stephen Decatur High School, he carried with him a secret desire to be a writer. With so much encouragement and support at home, along with Richard's respect for the rules and endless studying, he buckled down and performed well in school. Peck has said the following of his self-imposed rule: "I really thought you had a lot of dues to pay before they'd let you into adulthood . . . I believed it more than most."[14]

Asked later if he ever rebelled, he is quick to point out that he did not. "Oh, no. I thought rebellion was for people who could afford it. People who didn't have to get good grades because they didn't have to get a scholarship. People who could wreck their car because they

Richard Peck's senior portrait from his high school yearbook.

could get another one. No, I was more driven by life, and that too made a novelist out of me. Because a novel is always about the consequences of actions."[15] Because of his sharp, steady work ethic and study habits, he was welcomed into the National Honor Society.

It was not always easy for him in school. He did run across a tough cookie—Miss Franklin, his senior English teacher, who professed she had the power to stop him from entering the college of his choice. She wrote on his first homework assignment, "Never Express Yourself Again on My Time. Find a More Interesting Topic." She taught Peck a hard lesson—that material about himself was not interesting enough. Peck learned a lot and made it a point to take what adults said seriously.[16]

People who know Richard Peck comment on his eloquent speech and good manners. He admits he learned some of this etiquette at Miss Van Dyke's Fortnightly Dancing Class. This dancing class was a co-ed tradition in Decatur and taught by a "small, fierce woman in a black dress." Peck says the class was similar to a dancing "boot camp," where the waltz, fox trot, and rumba were learned "while in the very pit of puberty." Peck says, "On Saturdays I bagged groceries at the A&P for the wage of $7.45 which went farther then. A good deal of it went for wrist corsages, and I had the white dinner jacket by junior year."[17]

As a young man coming of age in a small country town, Richard pondered deeply about his future. He knew he wanted to work with words, but gender stereotypes were stronger then— becoming a writer was not considered a manly job to some people. He remembers being nervous about choosing a potential career path. "What didn't help was that I couldn't say I was going to be a writer, because boys were supposed to make livings. And so I said I was going to be a teacher, and that shut everybody up."[18]

Despite strong family ties, a beautiful Midwestern landscape, academic triumphs, and being lucky enough to have grown up in a loving home, Richard was born with "itchy feet"— somehow he had a gut feeling that real life was going on somewhere else.[19]

Richard daydreamed of eventually saying good-bye to the Illinois countryside. He was longing for the buzz and energy of the big city. His yearning to leave Decatur stirred fiery passions from within, but being a writer would have to wait a little while longer. College life beckoned, as did Uncle Sam and a wartime draft.

Chapter 3

University Days—and Wartime

Imagine being eighteen years old, fresh out of high school, and facing the chance of being drafted into war. This was reality in the early 1950s, the same time Peck was bound for college. The Korean War (1950–1953), a conflict between North Korea and South Korea, was in full tilt. The United States became involved when Democratic President Harry S. Truman heard about the surprise invasion of South Korea. The Americans stepped in to help stop the spread of communism. This act came with a high price—the military draft for American boys. The only way for young men to avoid the draft (at least temporarily) was to attend college.

It was a tense time for university students, and Peck felt the sting of it. The draft boards could ultimately decide the fates and futures of young men. The threat of the military draft loomed in Peck's mind. Attending college—and earning grades that would keep a student in the upper half of his class—was one of the few ways a male could avoid combat and perhaps even death. Almost thirty-three thousand United States soldiers were killed in action in the Korean War.

As Peck headed to college in 1952, to DePauw University in Greencastle, Indiana, any chance of going to war was delayed. He felt lucky that his immediate future was the safe campus soil of DePauw, and far away from enemy gunfire.

All that buckling down in high school started to pay off, and Peck began to reap the rewards of his previous academic work. He was named a Rector Scholar when he was admitted to DePauw. This scholarship was granted to exceptional DePauw students—those with outstanding academics and character. A scholarship in hand, Peck immersed himself in college life. He became a Delta Chi fraternity member and joined in with Greek life traditions—playing bridge, late-night coffee sipping after football games, singing songs around the baby grand piano that was in the Delta Chi house, and of course, cramming for tests in late-night study-fests. There were also dances to attend, under starry skies, with pretty, blonde-haired women.

Between the wild and crazy days of Greek life, the war raged on out in the "real world." Reality kept creeping back into view, even on campus. A senior in Peck's fraternity house let his grades slip below the college average and DePauw informed this student's hometown draft board. In an instant, the boy was sent to basic training at Fort Leonard Wood. It was a nerve-racking day for everyone who knew the boy. Peck and his classmates wondered if the same thing could happen to them too.[1]

In 1955, during his junior year, Peck fulfilled one of his boyhood dreams through the foreign study program at DePauw. He hopped aboard the *Ile de France* to spend a year in Europe studying abroad. In order to afford this privilege and fund the trip, he had worked as a dishwasher at George Williams College Camp on Lake Geneva, Wisconsin, the summer before. He managed to scrape together the $165 fare. Along with finding enough money, he also coaxed permission from the

Richard Peck relaxes in London in May 2005. As a young boy, Peck had dreamed of seeing Europe.

local draft board. They allowed him to leave the country for a year. The Army kept a close eye on men his age.[2]

The start of his adventure was something like a scene from an old movie. Peck remembers walking the gangplank onto the *Ile de France*. It was a massive ocean liner. And when it left the dock, ticker tape and streamers flew and swirled in the cool September air. The ship splashed down the Hudson River, taking Peck toward the cold Atlantic Ocean, and off toward a foreign world that Peck had longed to explore. Peck set sail, experiencing a bit of culture aboard the ship— French food, foreign films, and, according to French custom, a bathing ritual that baffled him. Baths had to be scheduled with the deck steward, and to complicate matters, he was to bathe in a tub of warm seawater while standing up in a sway-ing ship—a tricky move![3]

Once overseas Peck entered Exeter University, where he studied both British history and litera-ture during his yearlong stay in the town of Devon. He learned some European culture and made friends who came from all over the globe. There were less than a dozen American students there.

Peck also shed a bit of his American Mid-western accent while in Europe. He finally found a slice of what he yearned for—the thrill of faraway places. While at Exeter, he listened to differing opinions, learning that people from other countries see history differently. Peck later says that this taught him an example of point of view, which a novel needs to succeed.

Though Peck still had his eye on becoming a teacher, he had a towering hurdle to jump— something he had avoided dealing with his entire life—fear of public speaking. Peck admits to suffering horrible symptoms—a dry mouth and wobbly knees. He questioned his ability to become a teacher because he was too afraid to speak in front of a class. He faced this demon while at Exeter with the aid of his kind tutor, Professor Salter, who gave him an unusual "do-or-die" assignment.

One day, his professor coolly said, "The University is sending out to a local grammar school a panel of foreign students to speak about the educational systems of their countries. You will speak for the United States." Peck remembers donning his best suit and heading to the Blundell's School, where the speech was to be given. The audience was a blur of young faces. A classmate from Egypt spoke first, and did so with ease. Next, a man from Finland spoke who struggled with a heavy accent. Then came a staunch-speaking German, and finally an articulate French woman. Peck was last to speak. Somehow, through staring faces and an eerie silence, Peck made it through that nervous moment. Afterward he felt unchained, after hiding from his fear for so long. He was free to be on stage and relieved that teaching would be a part of his future after all.[4]

Exeter was a place where students wore

uniforms, toasted the Queen of England, and had the ability to speak some form of Latin. One place Peck was able to cut loose and relax was the dance floor. Despite the social stiffness that plagued his uptight British classmates, Peck had fun with other American students "tripping the light fantastic"—slang for dancing the night away.

Peck learned a lot about culture while in Europe. He saw plays in the London and Stratford theaters. He toured the countryside, catching a glimpse of Germany, where he would soon be stationed as a soldier. Seeing the continent of Europe strengthened Peck's love of far-off places and his curiosity in geography. He was swept away by views of the world. Some of his future readers

Richard Peck poses for a publicity photo alongside an ice cream truck in London.

might not ever get a chance to see these places—in person or on a classroom map.

Maybe this is why several years later many of Peck's novels contain a character who has a jaunt to a distant land, even if it is only from one part of the state to another. In the 2001 Newbery Medal winner, *A Year Down Yonder*, fifteen-year-old Mary Alice travels by train to a remote town in southern Illinois. And it feels like a world away from her hometown of Chicago.

When Peck finally cruised home on the *Queen Elizabeth*, he found the United States was mostly unchanged. He started his senior year of college at DePauw and focused on completing his education courses. In the background was life in the fraternity house—and the draft board and its emotional intimidation—but mostly regular life, people, and conversations were about the same as he had left it.

Peck says that his DePauw professors were challenging, which benefited him down the road when he began to create stories. "DePauw made a writer out of me," Peck has said. "It warned me never to show my rough draft to anybody. That helps. I write each of my books six times because I have to, and it's the sixth version my editor sees and nothing before that. I learned that from DePauw professors, who at that time had the authority to reject anything but your best work."[5]

He graduated from DePauw in 1956 with a bachelor's degree. Fast-forward four decades and in 1999 he was awarded their highest honor that a university can bestow—an honorary doctor of letters degree.

With the ink on his diploma barely dry, Peck was drafted into the Army and became a soldier. His stint in the Army officially began in the wee morning hours of the Decatur, Illinois, train station. He waited for the 4:00 A.M. train with a copy of *Moby Dick* under his arm. He did basic training in Colorado at Fort Carson in the frigid winter month of January. It was physically grueling. Besides learning how to shoot a gun at the firing range, he ran miles every morning in freezing temperatures, and once he marched fifty miles up a mountain in full gear. Mostly, he wished for heat. He lost twenty-five pounds. After basic training, he was shipped to a base in Ansbach (in what was then West Germany). Peck describes the town as a "sleepy Hansel-and-Gretel kind of place." He was assigned as a clerk/typist. He says, "I learned the advantages of literacy."[6]

Peck was relieved to learn that his writing skills would keep him off the front lines. "If you can type, spell, and improvise mid-sentence, you can work in a clean dry office near a warm stove [instead of being] knee-deep in a moist foxhole staring through barbed wire at an East German soldier who's staring back at you."[7]

As time went on, Peck began to think of advancement in the ranks. He had an epiphany one Sunday morning in the chapel while listening to a sermon. That very day, he marched back to his barracks and wrote a sermon of his own. Later he slid it under the door of the chaplain's office. The chaplain delivered Peck's sermon the following Sunday. Making a point to be seen the next time he slid a sermon under the chaplain's door, Peck was hired on the spot as the chaplain's assistant. Peck says, "Like a novel, a sermon needs to be for the congregation, not the preacher."[8]

Peck and the chaplain soon headed for a new post in Stuttgart, a wealthy and modern city. Surprisingly, Peck's new job in the Army expanded. Besides ghostwriting sermons, he also began conducting marriage-counseling sessions. He was "on call" a lot in the evenings. When soldiers saw a light on in the chapel, they would stop by and unload their troubles on Peck. In a warm, safe place, Peck honed his listening skills by hearing plenty of confessions.

He left the Army in 1958 after serving for two years. Now a man (but still a bookworm), he was ready to start a life on his own and career as a teacher.

Chapter 4

The English Teacher

Peck returned to the United States after his tour of duty in the Army. Back on Midwestern soil, he enrolled at Southern Illinois University (SIU) in Carbondale. In order to help pay for his master's degree at SIU, he struck a deal to serve as a teaching assistant in SIU's English department. This meant teaching freshmen composition a couple of evenings a week. Ironically, his first day of teaching ended up starting in the evening—night school, as it is commonly called. Although Peck was the professor, he was the youngest person in the room.

From his first group of adult students, he "learned the teacher's need to reassure." He had to assure his students over and over. He had to talk most of them out of dropping the course (or dropping out altogether) at one time or another because many of these adult students felt they had started too late in their life to try to graduate from college. Some thought they were too old. Most had day jobs, kids, and busy lives. Peck said of the experience, "Never again was I to know students this vulnerable or punctual. One night Mr. Ginganbach [one of Peck's students] barreled in an hour late." Mr. Ginganbach said, "I'd have been on time, but I had to take the wife to the labor room."[1]

After teaching at SIU for two years (1958–1960), Peck left to teach and do additional graduate work for one year at Washington University in St. Louis. But he eventually returned to his first game plan—to teach high school. Down deep, Peck knew the odds of becoming a writer and making a livable wage were slim. He says, "I'd come from Illinois where we were raised to make livings, not take chances." Peck admired teachers though, so he thought that becoming a teacher would be an acceptable second bet. Although he said he knew he had a novel in him, he was not yet ready to become a writer. So he put the idea out of his head. But this goal stayed inside his heart and mind, as dreams do, reminding him from time to time of what is possible.[2]

In 1961, Peck landed his first public high school teaching job at Glenbrook North High School in his home state of Illinois, a place just north of the busy city of Chicago. The city is Northbrook, and it is in the suburbs of Chicago.

Peck was slightly surprised at what he found there. He says of the kids who attended that school, "The students were strongly defended by peer grouping, hair spray, and family money. . . . Every parent expected college entrance for their child."[3]

Peck accepted the truth—that they were not like him, and he struggled with how to connect with them. He had a hard time reaching this new breed of teenagers. They were "overindulged, self-centered, unchallenged, and rootless."[4]

Perhaps some of the jarring experiences he had with wealthy suburban kids caused Peck to later set so many of his novels in the suburbs to try to reach this new generation. *Are You in the House Alone?* (Viking, 1976) was his emotional and disturbing novel that was set in the suburbs—a place Peck says is neither country nor city.

Are You in the House Alone? is a chilling novel about sixteen-year-old Gail, who is stalked and then raped. A boy in her peer group commits the crime. He is a classmate.

One of the novel's themes is that the victim also does a life sentence, regardless of whether the accuser is ever taken to court or convicted. In the story, everyone around Gail fails her, starting with the failure of the law, and including her family and friends. To make matters worse, almost everyone wants to put the tragedy behind him or her and forget it happened.

Statistics show that most rape cases go unreported. Often the attacker gets away with it. As

Richard Peck shows off his flashy socks in 2004. Peck sometimes used his sense of humor to connect with his students when he was a teacher.

she sits in the hospital just after the attack, Gail knows the shameful truth. She says, "I can't tell anybody. They won't believe me."[5]

Peck also set *Remembering the Good Times* (Delacorte, 1985) in the suburbs. This story is about teenage suicide. Peck says that the main character, Trav, is pushed over the edge by the pressures of high school and of what lies ahead for him as a grown-up. Trav is a boy "most likely to succeed," and he is driven by a desperation masked by his success. Trav chooses death because he does not believe he is being prepared for the challenge of adult life.

Peck's books are realistic, and maybe it is because of his time in the classroom, being with real kids up close and in person. The reader is immediately thrust into the action, as if he or she is an invisible friend standing alongside the main characters.

Some of his darker story ideas Peck was able to gather while a teacher, but if he was going to write about rape, unwanted pregnancy, or suicide—all potent and controversial topics—he had to know the ins and outs of these upsetting subjects in order to write with any sense of believability and emotional force. Unlike his later novels that are saturated with humor, the earlier "problem novels" required plenty of topical research.

Peck, although dismayed at Glenbrook, tried his best to teach the kids in this suburban Chicago high school. In the end, though, he had trouble dealing with the mindset of the teens and parents.

He became discouraged. He liked his students, but he compared his teaching job to a form of psychiatric social work, where school was less about learning and more about counseling and baby-sitting. He says that high school is a place where oftentimes parents and teachers never meet or talk. Peck says he tried hard to educate his students, but they ended up educating him. He says teaching there he received a crash course in his own future.[6]

Certainly, Peck's future novels would bear out many of the experiences he witnessed firsthand in the classroom. He saw many kids who had troubles—who learned lessons the hard way. Everything he saw later inspired dramatic plots. He noticed that, unlike in his own childhood, today's teens allow the authority of friends and peer groups to replace adult authority. Kids sometimes believe that they had better not become higher achievers than their buddies and class-mates. Peck maintains that, "You only grow up when you've walked away from those people. In all my novels, you have to declare your independence from your peers before you can take that first real step toward yourself."[7]

Many years after all of these classroom ordeals—battling shrinking attention spans, rowdy kids, and power struggles between students, parents, and administrators—Peck was inspired to write the poem "A Teacher's Prayer":

Oh God, I'm only a teacher,
   And it's lonely work because I'm the only member
   of my species in the room.

35

I like kids, and I love my subject matter,
And I have higher hopes for these kids of mine than
they have for themselves:
> I want them to create. They want to consume.
> I want them to love the world. They want the
> world to love them.
> I want every day to be different. They want every
> day to be the same.
> I want them to burn with zeal, about something.
> They want to be cool, about everything.
> I want them to think. They want me to tell them.
> I want the bell to ring. They want the bell to ring.

Oh God, I'm only a teacher,
> I'm not their buddy. I don't want to be. I've seen
> what they do to their buddies.
> I'm not their parent, and yet they're looking high
> and low for parents and can't seem to find them.
> I'm their teacher. I don't want them to take me at
> my word. I want them to find the words.

Oh God, I'm only a teacher,
> So I'm perfectly willing to move mountains if You'll
> send me some hands for my end of the lever:
>> Send me a couple of administrators who care more
>> about standards than they do about their jobs.
>> Send me the occasional parent who sees in me a
>> colleague, not a scapegoat.
>> Send me a few kids every semester willing to
>> brave their peers in order to learn.

Oh God, I'm only a teacher,
> I want to make bricks. Could you send me some
> straw?
> > Amen[8]

CHAPTER 5

A HiqHER CaLLiNq

Hfter teaching for two years at Glenbrook North High School, in 1963 Peck accepted a job as a textbook editor for Scott, Foresman and Company in Chicago. While there, he wrote a guide to Chicago nightlife, *Old Town: A Complete Guide: Strolling, Shopping, Supping, Sipping*, which he self-published in 1965 with a college friend.

Then finally, a childhood dream came true. In 1965, at the age of thirty-two, he moved to New York for a fresh start. He was offered a teaching job at Hunter College High School for academically gifted girls (grades 7–12). He had waited all his life to live in a place like New York, and he had finally received the call to come. It was his chance to be a part of "The City That Never Sleeps."

When he arrived in New York, he was amazed

to see that the faculty in the English department was removing *To Kill a Mockingbird*, Harper Lee's classic book about a small southern town and racism, from classes and courses. It was book banning, no matter what the excuse. In typical Peck style, he did the only logical thing. He told his students they were banned from reading it. It was a sly move on his part. All of them read *To Kill a Mockingbird* that semester.[1]

Peck remembers that many things went wrong that first year of teaching—what he called "omens." Once he was trapped for five hours in a subway car during a blackout. He, along with the other people who were stuck, was pulled out through a manhole. Peck later wrote a fictional account about it in his novel *Father Figure* (Viking, 1978).[2]

Peck did some moonlighting that first year, too. A colleague, Ned Hoopes, asked Peck to work together on a book with him. He did, and the project resulted in *Edge of Awareness: Twenty-Five Contemporary Essays* (Dell, 1966). Peck remembers receiving $730, which back then was two months' pay. Millions of copies of the book have been sold.[3]

Meanwhile, back at Hunter College, old frustrations showed up again. One aggravation Peck encountered was the attitude of his students calling themselves "gifted." He did not like a label that bigheaded, especially when his students used it against him. When Margaret Mead, a female anthropologist from the Natural History Museum, visited the school to talk to the senior girls, she suggested to the students that they also needed real-world skills—like nursing or secretarial training. Peck remembers one of his students jumping to her feet. She rudely proclaimed, "Lady, I don't think you know who we are. We aren't going to be secretaries. We're gifted!"[4]

As if his prior teaching post back in the suburbs of Chicago had not been disappointing enough, this new school all but did Peck in. He did all he could to reach these students. Once he stood on his desk and recited Mark Antony's fiery funeral oration from Shakespeare's *Julius Caesar*. Still, Peck felt his students were not interested. Maybe because too many other events were taking over outside the classroom.

It was the mid-1960s, and teens across America were becoming bold—less conservative in their behavior and dress. Rock 'n' roll came into its own. Overall, this was a time of heavy political activism. Social and cultural changes were taking root. Organized protests for civil rights sparked rioting among several groups. Women protested their "second-class" role in society, citing unequal pay for doing the same work. African Americans protested against mistreatment and racism in the workplace and schools. Many American teenagers questioned the government about why American troops were being sent to fight in the Vietnam War (1954–1975). Violent "peace" rallies erupted on campuses over the war. A common factor was that youth were a part of many of these activities.[5]

Richard Peck is photographed at the Arne Nixon Center for the Study of Children's Literature (located on the fourth floor of the Henry Madden Library at California State University, Fresno), where he gave a lecture in 2002.

Almost everywhere the country was changing and opinions were shifting. Some people called it a mess. Some people called it an attack on morals and values. Some people called it empowerment. A popular saying during this time was "Power to the people!"

It bothered Peck that many kids refused to take responsibility for their own actions. All Peck could do was stand by and watch the tide shift. Even worse, he felt like schools, teachers, and parents caved in and lost control. It was, as Peck says, "A massive failure of nerve."[6]

Peck refers to it as the "terrible 1960s." He says that near the end of that decade "the authority of the American family collapsed among all classes of people, and took the school system with it."[7]

Then, in 1969, he accepted a one-year fellowship as assistant director of the Council for Basic Education in Washington, D.C. This organization evaluated educational progress. While there, Peck learned how to be a working writer. He assisted with publications, worked on writing newsletters and articles, and even visited classrooms where he would sit and observe kids and the programs being taught to them.

When he returned to New York, he could no longer deny the aching inside. He *had* to be a writer. At least he had to try. The decision to leave teaching was easier because he had finally had enough of the crumbling standards of the education system anyway. He was not only burned out, but also exasperated.[8] He had witnessed an eighth-grade girl fall to the floor from a drug overdose. He had heard ramblings from "gifted" students who were above typing or going to the library to research. He compared teaching to "psychiatric social work."[9]

He says, "I noticed that the world of the young was a far more dangerous place than it had been for me back in the 1950s, when we were never more than five minutes from the nearest adult."[10]

When Peck realized he was not in control of the classroom, he believed that nothing would get better in teaching. He quit because he could no longer teach as he had been taught.[11]

Peck had taken all the madness he could stand, and he left teaching for good on May 24, 1971, immediately after the seventh-period bell. He went home to write . . . or die.

CHAPTER 6

WRITING FOR GENERATION "NEXT"

Peck jumped headfirst into writing for those students he had left behind in the classroom. He moved his typewriter out into the garden of the brick barn in Brooklyn where he lived. Peck's home was an 1830s-style carriage house in Brooklyn Heights, on the outskirts of New York City. He liked it there. His street reminded him of the Midwest, with its tree-lined landscape.[1]

It took courage to walk away from teaching with no backup plan, money, or insurance. Most authors began writing and kept their day jobs until their writing allowed them to be self-sufficient. It probably helped that he was not married and could dabble in this "change of life" experiment by himself. Even still, Peck knew he was taking a huge risk. (Add to that that he had not even tried writing fiction before!)

Now jobless and alone, and staring at the keys of his Royal Standard typewriter, he faced an uphill battle that summer—starting his first novel. He focused on writing for teenagers, because of his time as a teacher. He began furiously studying and reading other young adult authors' works. They were now his competition.

Peck had no choice but to make this pipe dream of his work. It was either write or die . . . and maybe even starve. He did not leave the house much during the time he was writing his first book, because he was afraid of spending money. He did not think about failure. He tried to stay in the present.

Another pesky problem staring him in the face was what to write about. He decided to write about a home for unwed teenage mothers, based on his friends Jean and Richard Hughes, who permitted unwed, pregnant girls to stay in their home. Peck struggled with viewpoint, and although he had taught viewpoint, using it the right way turned out to be a bit frustrating. At first, he tried to make the narrator the pregnant girl, but it did not feel right.

The project was not going as planned. Peck traipsed outside to the garden and sat under a weeping willow tree. Under the hot sun, he knew he was stuck in the middle of the story, without a clear idea of how to fix what was wrong. He scrapped what he had and started over from page one. He had decided that instead of the mother telling her own story, he would write it from the viewpoint of the pregnant girl's younger sister.[2]

Peck stayed holed up in his home for four months that hot summer tapping the typewriter keys. When he finally finished the manuscript, he carefully bundled his first work of fiction and placed it in a shoe box and toted it to the editor in chief of Holt, Rinehart and Winston, George Nicholson, an editor whom Peck had met years earlier and had formed a relationship with.[3]

Peck had no choice but to make this pipe dream of his work.

Peck was overwhelmed that evening—he had nothing to work on and nothing to write about. He walked to the edge of the city and then back home again, and fell into bed, never bothering to remove his clothes. The next morning, the phone rang at 8:30 A.M. It was George Nicholson calling to say, "You can start your second novel."

Despite the usual difficulty most authors experience trying to sell their first novel, Peck sold Don't Look and It Won't Hurt in 1971 to Holt, Rinehart and Winston in just one day. Selling a novel in twenty-four hours is almost unheard of in the publishing industry. Usually it takes months, or even years, for a writer to land that coveted first contract. Not only did Peck sell his first novel quickly, but he also formed a dynamic relationship with George Nicholson, who went on to publish many of Peck's young adult novels.

During the early days of Peck's budding writing career, he had to learn a few new skills, one of which was learning how to be alone all day. Another was a way to find extra cash, to cover his living expenses. He wrote articles for the *New York Times*, *Saturday Review*, and *House Beautiful*.

Peck was also commissioned to write a series of young adult book reviews, where he spoke about the controversial book written by Robert Cormier (1925–2000)—*The Chocolate War* (Knopf Books for Young Readers, 1974). It is a story about Jerry

Richard Peck with Denise Sciandra, president of Arne Nixon Center for the Study of Children's Literature, in 2002.

Renault, a high school freshman at Trinity School, and his refusal to sell chocolates for his school fund-raiser. Jerry ponders the question, "Do I dare disturb the universe?" Along the way, he bucks the secret society (the Vigils club), which causes all heck to break loose. It causes a full-blown social war at the school.

Due to its controversial content, *The Chocolate War* was ranked fourth on the American Library Association's *100 Most Frequently Challenged Books* of 1990–2000. It is still under fire even though the book was written over thirty years ago. As recently as 2005, it has been on the American Library Association's "most-challenged" book list. The book usually draws complaints from parents, and others, concerned about its sexual content, offensive language, religious viewpoint, and violence. Peck, on the other hand, says *The Chocolate War* is one of the best novels of the last fifty years.

In short order, schools, teachers, and librarians started calling Peck. They wanted him to come speak to the young about writing. With just one novel underfoot, he was asked to speak at the Indiana Library Association. He prepped his speech for a month, trying to memorize every word. A little bit of nerves and self-doubt inched into his head before he was due to start talking to the kids, parents, and guests who had gathered to hear him. But when he finished speaking, forty-five minutes after he began, he realized he had not even turned the page on his script.

He says, "I'd subconsciously memorized it all, and adrenaline did the rest."[4]

Between travels, he wasted no time getting back to his typewriter. He began writing two more novels for young people. His next works were *Dreamland Lake* and *Through a Brief Darkness*. Although he had other genres of work published, including a collection of essays and various articles, his true love was writing for the young. In 1974, Peck's fourth novel, *Representing Super Doll*, was published. Peck noted, "The years and the books roll on."[5]

Peck spends most of his days juggling writing projects against school and library visits with the young. He travels thousands of miles and even overseas to find them. Before he meets face-to-face with kids, he usually asks students to write a paper for him before he arrives—something

> **"The years and the books roll on."**
>
> **—Richard Peck**

that he can read in advance. He asks the students to write an essay with the title "Something that Happened to Me That Would Fit into a Novel." He receives papers that contain a variety of topics. Most are about death, divorce, or drugs. Some are romances, comedies, or science fiction. Peck knows that some of the stories he receives did not *really* happen to the authors of the papers, but that is okay. The point is for the students to write, and Peck wins because sometimes he finds his next story idea in one of these essays.

Some of the students who send him papers are aspiring writers, and Peck gives them feedback. Peck says there is no foolproof formula for good writing, but he has been asked so often about the rules of writing that he finally wrote down a list of eight tips. In his usual style, some of his suggestions are tongue-in-cheek. It is highly likely that Peck learned some of these "lessons" the hard way—by practice, time spent in the classroom when he was a teacher, and being a passionate reader. (Having a healthy streak of writing talent helped too!)

Other advice he has for budding writers is to learn five new words a day; to read the kinds of books that you want to write; to figure out how the author wove the story together; and to visit the local library often and look for treasures there— make friends with librarians![6]

During the 1970s, 1980s, and 1990s, Peck wrote novel after novel for young people and adults, and he even made time to pen a collection of poems, essays, and short stories. He began to carve out a name for himself in the book publishing industry. Some of his books were turned into movies. Peck writes about a novel per year for kids. He has taken only a brief detour here or there to write a handful of poems and books for the adult audience.

One of his most popular teen characters is Blossom Culp. He wrote three books about her, the first one being *The Ghost Belonged to Me*. Blossom has the ability to see into the future.

Richard Peck has attributed most of the booming success he has had as a writer to two things: a mother who read to him, and his teaching career. With millions of books in print and much financial success, you would think that he had reached the pinnacle of his writing career. But the best was yet to come . . . Grandma Dowdel was about to play a starring role and change his life forever.

CHAPTER 7

The Newberys and the White House

Peck says that Grandma Dowdel came to life because of a challenge put forth by a fellow writer. This man was Harry Mazer. In 1995, Mazer invited some of his writing colleagues to come up with a short story for an anthology he was creating. The hitch was that the stories had to be about guns. Yes . . . guns! It was an unconventional theme for a children's book, to say the least. Peck secretly wondered how the subject matter would be received with librarians, yet he was up for the challenge. Peck accepted Mazer's offer to write the story about guns, but "itched" to send Mazer a postcard that said, "Yes, I'll give it a shot."[1]

Except Peck did not have a trigger-happy finger. His mind was forced to drift back to the last time he had fired a gun. His brainstorming took him back to the year 1957, returning him to the rifle range at Fort Carson, Colorado. The last time he had fired a gun he was a young man—a soldier in the Army.[2]

Wanting to write something a bit different for the anthology, he settled on an absurd, granny-like character: a woman with a 12-gauge double-barreled Winchester shotgun entered his mind. Little did he know at the time that Grandma Dowdel would change his life forever. Peck called his story "Shotgun Cheatham's Last Night Above Ground." The book was eventually titled *Twelve Shots* (Laurel Leaf, 1998).

Peck also showed this gun story to his then-editor at Dial books, Cindy Kane. She told Peck that he should write an entire book about Grandma Dowdel. He did, and the book became *A Long Way from Chicago* (Dial, 1998). The novel is set during the Great Depression and is format-ted as eight episodes spanning the years 1929 through 1942. The fifteen-year-old narrator of the stories is Joey Dowdel. Joey and his younger sister, Mary Alice, both city kids from Chicago, are sent downstate for regular visits with Grandma Dowdel, a woman famous for having things her own way and, at the very least, stretching the truth. *Publisher's Weekly* describes Grandma Dowdel as, "A woman as 'old as the hills,' 'tough as an old boot,' and larger than life."[3]

A neat feature of the book is that a reader can learn history while enjoying the story. The teacher in Peck, of course, is a big believer in knowing history and geography.

After the book's publication, Peck received the call that every writer would love to receive, but most never expect to come: The Newbery committee called to inform him that he had been awarded a Newbery Honor for *A Long Way from Chicago*.

Letters about Grandma poured in. Peck says, "The letters came in at once: 'Was she YOUR grandmother?' they ask. Did my own grandmother fire off both barrels of a shotgun in her own front room? Did she pour warm glue on the head of a hapless Halloweener? Did she spike the punch at a DAR (Daughters of the American Revolution) tea? Well, no." Grandma Dowdel was larger-than-life—on both the pages of the book and in Peck's real life—and in the lives of his readers.[4]

Peck says, "Young readers need stories of rugged individualism because most of them live in a world completely ruled by peer-group conformity." Grandma Dowdel embodies independence. Maybe that is why she is so popular with teenagers. "She isn't an old lady at all. Maybe she's a teenager in disguise. After all, she believes the rules are for other people. She always wants her own way. Sounds like adolescence to me, and even more like puberty."[5] Peck has had wise, elderly role models in his novels before, but the feisty Grandma Dowdel made the biggest splash.

Since the book received the Newbery Honor in 1999, his editor did the only logical thing: She told him to write *another* book about Grandma

Richard Peck enjoys being chauffeured in a classic car in October 2004. Many of Peck's stories are set in (or evoke) an older, classic era of U.S. history.

Dowdel. Peck did as he was told and began writing a sequel. The result was *A Year Down Yonder* (Dial, 2000). This time Joey's younger sister, Mary Alice, tells the story. The setting again is a fictionalized town not mentioned by name, but Peck admits that it is based on his childhood memories with his grandparents around Cerro Gordo, Illinois, a rural town in Southern Illinois. Not naming the town in both books was intentional. Peck wants his readers to imagine that Cerro Gordo is their own small town, or a small town they know. For Peck, Cerro Gordo, Illinois, is the home of his grandparents, and he draws on his memories of visits to the area.[6]

A Year Down Yonder is set in 1937. Mary Alice's parents lose their home in Chicago so she is sent to live with Grandma for a year. The feisty Grandma Dowdel is up to her old scheming ways, embarking on many a wild rampage. Best of all, the effect is good, old-fashioned, sidesplitting laughter. Mary Alice learns (as does the reader) that beneath Grandma's fibs and quirkiness there is a wonderful person with a big heart (not to mention a big dress size).

A Year Down Yonder was very popular. Many of Peck's readers claim to know Grandma Dowdel and what part of the country she lives in. He says, "I get letters every week from people who say, 'Grandma Dowdel is from down south! Grandma Dowdel is a Texan, isn't she?' I always say, 'If you want her to be, yes.' Southern traditions probably came up to my part of the state of Illinois. I think Southerners and Midwesterners merge nicely. The fact that we had the war probably makes us think we're more different than we are."[7]

Here is an excerpt of Grandma Dowdel in action, taking vengeance on a boy who has trespassed on her property in hopes of turning over her outdoor privy:

> Grandma lunged. As big as the cob house doorway, she surged through it. Moonlight struck her snow-white hair, and she looked eight feet tall. She'd have given a coroner a coronary. As the fallen boy raised his dazed head, she turned the pan of glue over on it. The glue was cool now and would set later.[8]

No matter where Grandma Dowdel really hails from—North, South, East, or West—she has struck a chord in the hearts of Peck's fanbase and book lovers across the globe. His fans are not only kids and teens, but also moms, dads, and senior citizens! *A Year Down Yonder* spans the generations because it is a tale where comedy and adventure collide head-on for readers of every age to enjoy. No matter where or when a good story is set, or the age of the characters, funny is funny.

It is no big surprise what happened next: It was a frosty early morning in January like any other. Peck was lying in bed. The telephone rang, and a voice on the other end of the line told him, "This is Caroline S. Parr of the Newbery committee calling you from the Midwinter American Library Association meeting in Washington, D.C. Your book, *A Year Down Yonder*, has won the 2001 Newbery Medal." Peck said, "Would you repeat that?" He heard a cheer in the background. He was stunned, but he was certainly awake. It was the call of a lifetime.[9]

Once the word was out, his phone did not quit ringing. Newspaper, magazine, and television reporters swarmed him. The news made him an instant star. The next day, he was a guest on the *Today* show with then-host Katie Couric.

As part of his acceptance speech Peck joked, "It has taken me a long time to find the key that unlocks a Newbery: a naked woman and a snake!"[10]

Fame brought with it some other major perks. On September 8, 2001, Peck traveled to the nation's capital and to the White House. Peck had

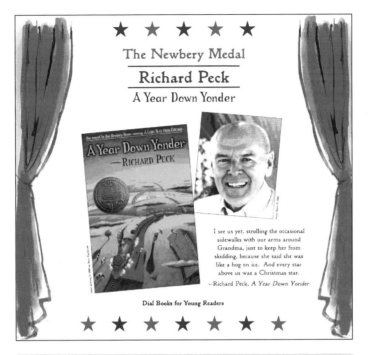

A page from the 2001 Newbery Award Banquet program.

been invited to participate in the first National Book Festival, hosted by First Lady Laura Bush. He was one of sixty authors featured, reading from his work under a tent on the grounds of the Library of Congress and the United States Capitol.

Basking in the glow of this exciting event, how could anyone have known what devastation and terror would soon arrive?

Days after the National Book Conference, terrorists intent on harming Americans flew two jumbo passenger airlines into the World Trade

Center towers. Within hours, the destroyed buildings collapsed. Many people died that day. A saddened Peck expressed his thoughts on the 2001 terrorist attack against America through the poem "September 11":

> We thought we'd outdistanced history—
> Told our children it was nowhere near;
> Even when history struck Columbine,
> It didn't happen here.
>
> We took down the maps in the classroom,
> And when they were safely furled,
> We told the young what they wanted to hear,
> That they were immune from a menacing world.
>
> But history isn't a folded-up map,
> Or an unread textbook tome;
> Now we know history's a fireman's child,
> Waiting at home alone.[11]

Everything was uncertain, and for a time, Americans, waving flags and participating in other such unifying events, bonded in a renewed patriotic camaraderie with a fervor not seen since the end of World War II. Peck described the attack as a wake-up call. But was it only temporary? Peck had hoped that new curriculums and new challenges would be developed, including, as he says, "the serious study of history and geography and government and foreign language."[12] He was pessimistic that such a change would happen though.

The following year, in a special ceremony at the White House on the evening of April 22, 2002, Richard Peck was awarded the 2001 National Humanities Medal by President George W. Bush. During the evening gala and awards presentation,

Richard Peck with his Newbery Medal stands in the Blue Room of the White House with President George W. Bush and First Lady Laura Bush.

the President of the United States declared, "Richard Peck has written more than twenty-five novels for younger readers which stress the importance of taking responsibility for one's actions. Major, please read the citation."

> Richard Peck, for writing books that inspire independence, courage, and strength of character in young adults.[13]

President Bush took the medal and placed it around Peck's neck. Peck beamed with humble pride, as he stood arm in arm with the President and First Lady. And for good reason: Peck was the first children's author to receive this honor.

Peck says, "I was surprised and delighted because in Mrs. Bush we have our first librarian First Lady." He admires the work Laura Bush has done to encourage reading and literacy, and he said that it was her choice to make him the first children's writer to receive this award.[14]

Although a map indicates that New York City is a long way from Decatur, Illinois, Peck's writing flair of "keeping it real" is rarely out of sync with his Midwestern roots. Many of Peck's books, much like his Newbery books, have a bold, wise (and sometimes kooky), elderly character, who is there to provide guidance to a teen.

A long time has passed since his first night as an inexperienced writer—that lonely evening in 1971, when he was riddled with self-doubt and without a "real" job. The Newberys were a defining high point in his writing career. The Newbery Medal is the top prize in children's literature. This kind of praise will keep his books on the library shelves for decades.

Peck is a famous person in the literary world, but he does not let that fact slow him down and he does not become conceited about his status. He does what he does best. He continues to write, about one novel per year, using the same Royal Standard typewriter and painstaking revision process. He writes each of his books six times, and when he completes a full first draft of a manuscript, he trashes the first chapter and writes an entirely new and different first chapter—the *real* first chapter. If he is not writing, he is at the library researching his next novel, or on a road trip visiting with kids.

CHAPTER 8

A LITERARY MAVERICK

Richard Peck's writing and revising process is unique. He writes his novels six times. He writes from first page to last page. Sure, like all authors and writers, he gets stuck sometimes, but he just goes back and works on an earlier scene until he is able to overcome the block. When he reaches the end of his novel, he trashes the first chapter, no matter how long he has worked on it. "Now that I know how the story ends, I can write a new first chapter." He does this because now that he knows the ending, he can write the *best* first chapter. Peck says, "The first chapter is the last chapter in disguise."

Peck also found—although it happened rather by accident—that he could write a punchy short story. He says, "I hadn't meant to be a short-story writer. I'd hoped to be Mark Twain. The first of his books to lift me out of my world and into a bigger one was *Life on the Mississippi*." He says that junior-high teaching gave him that flash of inspiration he needed to write a good short story. "When I was an English teacher, my students preferred fiction to reality. They were in junior high school, and so they preferred ANYTHING to reality." Even though Peck had novels in mind when he quit teaching to become a writer, he admits that, "A writer has to be ready to turn on a dime."[1]

> "I'd hoped to be Mark Twain."
>
> —Richard Peck

His first short-story assignment came from an unexpected phone call back in the late 1970s. Peck remembers being hunched over his typewriter when the phone rang. It was an editor of a magazine for teenagers on the other end of the telephone line. She asked him to write a short story, but it had to be set in junior high/middle school. He told her, "I don't do short stories." She said the pay was three hundred dollars. He agreed. The last thing she told Peck was, "It has to be very short . . . and it needs to end with a bang . . . we'll need it by Thursday."[2]

Peck had just thirty-six hours to write his first short story. The result was "Priscilla and the Wimps." The story is about Priscilla Roseberry and how she deals with the mighty bully of the school,

Monk Klutter. Monk gets what is coming to him—from a *girl*, no less. The story ends with a pop—an amazing, glorious twist of fate that all kids, especially the underdogs who are picked on—get a kick out of.

Peck's first short story opened new doors for him. He learned he could sometimes detour into this genre. Kids and teachers are still reading the story of Priscilla even today.

Fortune has a way of revealing itself in strange and unexpected ways. A few of Peck's short stories inspired award-winning novels. *A Long Way from Chicago* and *A Year Down Yonder* began as a tale

Cindy Kane, Richard Peck, and Lauri Hornik (left to right) at a Newbery dinner held in San Francisco in 2001.

called "Shotgun Cheatham's Last Night Above Ground." His novel *Fair Weather* (Puffin Books, 2001) was inspired by "The Electric Summer." All of his short stories are now published in a collection called *Past Perfect, Present Tense* (Dial Books, 2004).

Peck's other writing detours included a handful of novels for adults including *Amanda/Miranda* (Viking, 1980), *New York Time* (Delacorte, 1981), *This Family of Women* (Delacorte, 1983), and *London Holiday* (Penguin Putnam, 1998).

But novel writing for teenagers is his first love, so that is what he has spent most of his time doing. His earlier works for teens were labeled "problem novels" because they dealt with serious topics like death, suicide, rape, and pregnancy. Though Peck's books are expertly written, sometimes advocacy groups or a misguided parent has knocked the subject matter. Some people have even tried to censor his work. Censorship is a pet peeve of Peck's. Censorship is the practice of banning a book, and that disturbs him a lot.

Over the years, Peck has had many battles with censorship. Peck's Blossom Culp series was the target of attacks with critics citing the mention of the occult and contact with the dead. Peck says that the movement of public schools to ban "supernatural stories, Halloween decorations, and witchcraft" is seen as the attempt of the religious right to control public schools.[3]

In the mid-1980s, he once ran into the mother of a thirteen year old who refused to let her daughter read *Father Figure*. This parent also managed to have the book snatched off the library bookshelf. The mother criticized the suicide of the fictional mother in the novel. She also protested the issue of divorce and the back talking of the fictional son to his father.

The controversy of censorship fueled his fire. Peck became so passionate about book banning, especially after would-be censors attacked some of his own books, that he decided to write a novel about it. Peck dealt with the issue in his novel *The Last Safe Place on Earth* (Delacorte, 1995). This story is about censorship and religious extremism.

"Book censorship isn't about books . . ."
—Richard Peck

"Book censorship isn't about books; it comes of redirected parental fear," he says.[4] "I want to write novels that ask honest questions about serious issues. A novel is never an answer; it's always a question."[5]

About other censored authors, Peck says that Judy Blume's *Are You There God? It's Me, Margaret* is "arguably the first successful attempt in human history to give honest aid and comfort to girls embarking upon the physical and emotional ordeal of puberty. A generation later, Judy Blume still takes heat from book-burning mothers, her crime being that she is making contact with their daughters just as they are losing it."[6]

Peck's recent books are far less controversial, and they focus on the past. The characters speak a language with a heavy accent that dates back to the olden days—the nineteenth or early twentieth centuries. *The River Between Us* (Dial Books, 2003) is a story told mostly from the point of view of fifteen-year-old Tilly Pruitt. Peck writes about the conflicts of the Civil War, racism, and social squabbling. This book won the 2004 Scott O'Dell Historical Fiction Award.

In an earlier novel, *Fair Weather*, he makes thirteen-year-old Rosie Beckett's lively adventure and trip to see the 1893 Chicago's World Fair seem factual—as if it really happened. He mentions the *Farmer's Almanac* and the details of how an American family of that time period truly lived. He also puts historical figures like Buffalo Bill Cody (1846–1917) and singer-actress Lillian Russell (1861–1922) into a couple of scenes. Peck says, "I weave all my historical fiction around real events. And since my own favorite reading is biography, I take

Richard Peck is photographed holding one of his popular books in May 2005.

great pleasure in giving roles to the real people who lived in that time. Virtually every famous person of the time—political, theatrical, musical—appeared at the fair."[7]

Is it funny to write about the death of a teacher? In a tongue-in-cheek and folksy writing style, Peck makes it hilarious. The result is *The Teacher's Funeral: A Comedy in Three Parts* (Dial Books, 2004). It is 1904 in rural Indiana, and fifteen-year-old Russell has his hands full when his mean, curmudgeonly teacher dies (and he gets his hopes up too soon that the school will close, only to later have them squashed) and he finds out that his sister will take over as school-marm! Peck again steps back into the past and writes a tale that keeps his readers chuckling.

The Teacher's Funeral won the 2005 Christopher Award for Children's Books. Not being able to get enough of the graveyard and the deaths of school administrators, he follows this with a companion volume, *Here Lies the Librarian* (Dial Books, 2006).

Richard Peck is presently working on a book titled *On the Wings of Heroes*, and it is a work about his father. The novel is set during World War II, which were his grade school years. Peck says, "It is the portrait of my father I hope to get down on paper." *On the Wings of Heroes* is scheduled to be published in March 2007.

Peck admits to struggling with titles. Peck said that *A Year Down Yonder* is often misquoted as *A Year Down Under*. He says there is no perfect title except *Gone with the Wind*. (And, it is already taken!) He says he will make long lists to try to figure out what his title should be, but ultimately he tries to name the book from a line in the story because then it is easier to answer a popular question that kids normally ask him: "Where did you get the title?"[8]

Peck never fully walked away from teaching. For more than a decade, he has been adjunct faculty at Louisiana State University's School of Library and Information Science. He has taught courses on young adult services with LSU colleague and friend Patsy Perritt. There is a scholarship set up in his name to help librarians who are pursuing careers in youth services.[9]

> **Peck never fully walked away from teaching.**

Never accused of being boring or idle, his teaching gigs have taken him all over the globe. He was once a guest lecturer and creative writing instructor on cruise ships that sailed to international cities and ports.

In 2005, he joined a delegation of authors and traveled to Russia to participate in Ludmila Putin's book festival. (She is the wife of Russian President Vladimir Putin.) This festival was modeled after First Lady Laura Bush's National Book Festival. Peck says, "It was a very high moment in my career to meet Russian teachers and young people. My books are not translated there, and now I wish they were. It is a country waking up after a seventy-year nightmare. Moscow was one of the most exciting places I've ever been."

This was Peck's first visit to Moscow. He said it was very exciting and fun to be part of the delegation led by the Librarian of Congress. "I have been very lucky that my career, shall we say, is coming to its conclusion at the same time the First Lady of the land is a librarian!"[10]

Throughout his career, Peck has been flooded with boatloads of literary honors and countless awards. In 1977, his home state crowned him Illinois Writer of the Year. He twice won the Edgar Allan Poe Award (given by the Mystery Writers of America).

In 1990, Peck was given the American Library Association's Margaret A. Edwards Award, which honors an author's body of work and recognizes an author's efforts in helping teens become aware of themselves and addressing questions about their role and importance in relationships, society, and in the world. He was honored for the body of work that included *Are You in the House Alone?*, *Father Figure*, *The Ghost Belonged to Me*, *Ghosts I Have Been*, *Remembering the Good Times*, and *Secrets of the Shopping Mall*.

The award that changed his life forever was also from the American Library Association, which honored him in 2001 as the author of the most distinguished contribution to American literature for children—the prestigious John Newbery Medal for *A Year Down Yonder*. The year prior, he received the Newbery Honor for *A Long Way from Chicago*.

Another momentous award was the National Humanities Medal. Many of his books have been named ALA Notable Children's Books or ALA Best Books for Young Adults. Some have won, or been a finalist for, the National Book Award. You would be hard-pressed to find a publication or a children's writing association that has not recommended his books or singled them out for an award.

Several of Peck's books have been made into movies. They include

- *Are You in the House Alone?* (television movie), CBS, 1978
- *Child of Glass* (television movie based on *The Ghost Belonged to Me*), Walt Disney Productions, 1978
- *Father Figure* (television movie), Time-Life Productions, 1980
- *Gas Food Lodging* (major motion picture), Cineville International, 1992 (based on Peck's novel, *Don't Look and It Won't Hurt*)

Peck has been a vibrant author for almost forty years. He has spent his adult life targeting young adult readers and making an impact on youth, parents, writers, and others. He has written about social issues, ghosts, peer pressures, and, lately, an American past that is saturated with humorous, quirky characters. His body of work totals almost forty books.

Approaching what is traditionally regarded as retirement age (but showing no signs of retiring his typewriter), Peck seems to have endless stories in his mind. Now in his mid-seventies, he is still churning out a new book about every year. Although his most recent stories are set back in time, they still strike a familiar chord in the young person who reads them. Besides tickling their funny bone, Peck revives the past in a captivating way for present-day kids to discover and enjoy. He has a knack for inventing spunky characters both young and old, but also making the past seem glorious—maybe even a better place to live than the here and now.

CHAPTER 9

A TEACHER AT HEART

Richard Peck never totally left the classroom—he is still a teacher at heart, and his spirit lingers in the schoolhouse. Of course, good teachers always have lesson plans in mind. So he travels the globe visiting schools and libraries to talk to young readers, teachers, and librarians. Peck makes these long trips partly as motivation. He is looking for a story that will become his next book. He says, "For inspiration, I now travel about sixty thousand miles a year, on the trail of the young. Now, I never start a novel until some young reader, somewhere, gives me the necessary nudge."[1]

He also has a passion for reading, and he strives to inspire others. Parents are an important group he wants to reach. Parents are the foundation of a good education, Peck believes. Reading aloud and reading together is an important part of learning. For parents, Peck wrote the poem "Twenty Minutes a Day":

> Read to your children
> Twenty minutes a day;
> You have the time,
> And so do they.
>
> Read while the laundry is in the machine;
> Read while the dinner cooks;
> Tuck a child in the crook of your arm
> And reach for the library books.
>
> Hide the remote,
> Let the computer games cool,
> For one day your child will be off to school;
> "Remedial"? "Gifted"? You have the choice;
> Let them hear their first tales
> In the sound of your voice.
>
> Read in the morning;
> Read over noon;
> Read by the light of
> *Goodnight Moon.*
>
> Turn the pages together,
> Sitting close as you'll fit,
> Till a small voice beside you says,
> "Hey, don't quit."[2]

Peck created a list of seven "Dos and Don'ts" for parents who want their children to read. Number two on the "Do" list is, "Read aloud to children as much as you can, and don't stop even after they can read for themselves. Books are bonds between you and them." And number two on the "Don'ts" list is, "Never imply by word or attitude that reading and writing (including letter writing) is women's work."[3]

Peck also has strong opinions about the struggles and burdens the young are facing today. And rightly so, having been a teacher for so long and seeing so much turmoil in the classroom. Peck knows that kids *must* get an education. He says, "Only readers have futures—that if you cannot use language, it will be used against you—that if you cannot read appreciatively, write coherently, speak persuasively, and listen skeptically, you will find a way to fail at whatever you want." One of his most repeated mantras is "Nobody but a reader ever became a writer."[4]

A theme in most of his books is that young people can never begin to grow up until they experience independence from their peers. He is also quick to point out "that most truly successful men and women were not high-school hotshots, beauty queens, super jocks, or manipulative gang leaders."[5]

Peck also spends large chunks of his time encouraging aspiring children's writers. He is a member of the Society of Children's Book Writers and Illustrators (SCBWI) and has been a guest lecturer at many of their conferences, and he has led workshops on the craft of writing. SCBWI is an international organization (based in Los Angeles, California) for people who write, illustrate, or share a passionate interest in children's literature. There are presently more than nineteen thousand members worldwide. It the largest organization in the world dedicated to supporting children's writers and artists.

In 2004, Peck was named SCBWI's Member of the Year. They praised him for being "a tireless booster of the SCBWI as well as an eager volunteer in aiding the education and development of the children's book artistic community."[6]

Despite his amazing lifelong literary achievements, honors, and awards, and the glowing praise for his books, Peck still has to put in the long hard hours necessary to create his masterpieces. He does not skimp on his writing process. Even now, he writes all of his novels six times, and he does not use a computer to do so. He is still a fan of the typewriter.

Writing an excellent, true-to-life, historical novel requires more than family memories to spark ideas. Peck must dive into research at the library to create believable settings and characters. "I do endless research," he says. Before writing *A Year Down Yonder*, he read every issue of *Time* magazine in 1937 starting with January 1. He mapped out a timeline. He looked at clothing catalogs of the day (Lane Bryant and Montgomery Ward) because they listed prices for things. The historical research keeps the story believable, while his flair for "spinning your wheels" keeps the story entertaining.[7]

If something about Peck's writing style sounds familiar, it is no accident. There was a famous writer from the American Midwest, long before Peck, who was the all-time master of harmonizing

Peck at the "Dinosaurs of Waterhouse Hawkins" exhibit in London.

character, story, wit, and setting—Mark Twain (1835–1910). Mark Twain knew how to capture an audience. So does Peck. Twain charmed readers all over the world by writing stories of boyhood adventure, laced with hilarious scenes and colloquial language. So has Peck.

Peck says, "There's a debt I owe to the Midwest, to Mark Twain, and the great river that has nurtured my writing."[8] Twain's most famous characters are of course Tom Sawyer and Huckleberry Finn. Ernest Hemingway once said: "All modern American literature comes from one book by Mark Twain called [*Adventures of*] *Huckleberry Finn* . . . all American writing comes from that. There was nothing before. There has been nothing as good since."[9]

Peck's editor at Dial Books for Young Readers, Lauri Hornik, agrees with the comparison of Peck to Twain.

> I know that he is inspired by Mark Twain. There's something very Twain-esque about his settings, characters, and humor. He's satirical in that way and sort of exaggerates characters for comic effect to show us our foibles. We see through these exaggerated characters what is a little bit ridiculous in all of us. So there's that, and he's writing about historical settings, writing back in time is something he's been focusing on lately. He has such a feel for it that he has just found his stride with this historical and pastoral kind of setting.[10]

By today's standards, Peck is an old-fashioned man, with "old school" tendencies. He champions good behavior, manners, and courtesy. He despises technology when it takes the place of politeness. He looks down on cell phone chatter in public. He thinks video games are overused. "Television kills imagination," he has said. And what about e-mail? That may be the worst offender of all. With dramatic scorn, he says, "E-mail . . . when you don't care enough to send the very best." Sure, Peck is sarcastic about the pitfalls of electronic gadgets, but he is authentic and true to himself. He has opinions and is not afraid to express them.[11]

Peck is a neat dresser too. He usually wears conservative but stylish clothing. He is tall and slender, and he stands with good posture. He is sharp and clever in his speeches, and sometimes challenging, but also comes across as playful. He is famous for his punchy one-liners, affectionately known as "Peck-isms." For example, "Watching television is what you do with your life when you don't want to live it."

One thing is sure: Richard Peck has a way with words. He finds these words in family lore, through people he meets, from the places he has visited during his lifetime, during grueling days sitting in front of a typewriter at the writing desk of his New York apartment, and by spending long hours reading and researching the dark dusty archives of the library.

Some of those faraway places were no farther than his backyard in Decatur, Illinois. Wherever the story may unfold, he tells it with a hearty dose of style. His rural upbringing and eccentric relatives continue to fuel many of the settings and characters for his profoundly funny, real, and surprising stories. He has written some of the best children's novels of our time, and the best is yet to come.

As Peck matures, he is blossoming into one of the great writers of young adult literature. As one critic in the *Washington Post* said of Peck's writing, "He is among a handful of authors writing for pre-and-early teen readers, whose books are so quirkily original, so airily intelligent that a single paragraph can make a jaded reviewer's spirits rise."[12]

If the prior books are any indicator, Peck will continue to write best-selling books that reach millions of people. He says, "I'll go on bootlegging

Richard Peck relaxes with fellow author Will Hobbs and a canine companion.

history and geography in all my stories, tales of grandmas' houses with the privies standing proudly behind; tales lit and warmed by laughter and coal-oil lamplight, written in a twenty-first century lit by lightning."[13]

Between the crinkled, dog-eared pages of all good books, you start to believe as Richard Peck does, that there is a time-tested wonderment in what a story can be.

A story is a doorway
    That opens on a wider place;
A story is a mirror
    To reflect the reader's face.
A story is a question
    You hadn't thought to ponder;
A story is a pathway,
    Inviting you to wander.
A story is a window,
A story is a key,
A story is a lighthouse,
Beaming out to sea.
A story's a beginning;
    A story is an end;
And in the story's middle,
    You might just find a friend.[14]

"I want young people to know that in a book you can go anywhere and be anybody," Peck says. "I like writing about different times and different people, because I am still finding friends in books myself."[15]

In His Own Words

The following interview with Richard Peck was conducted by Kimberly Campbell via phone on Thursday, January 19, 2006, between 3:30 and 4:00 P.M.

Tell me about your most vivid memory as a child.

My beginning was a mother who read to me. That turned me in this direction before I went to school. And then discovering Mark Twain who spoke the language I heard in the middle west. From him I learned that you didn't have to be English, or from New England. That helped. What didn't help was that I couldn't say I was going to be a writer, because boys were supposed to make livings. And so I said I was going to be a teacher, and that shut everybody up.

I became an English teacher, as you know. I learned something every day of my teaching that led to a career in writing.

How has your family and their personalities influenced your writing?

They are Midwestern people at the end of a puritan tradition. And they don't tell their secrets but they'll tell yours. It wasn't a storytelling family, but it was a family with secrets. And that was more interesting. It made me do my own research. All families have secrets. Ours weren't very exciting, but they were ours. We had a kind of privacy you don't see in a later generation, and in this part of the country. I think coming from the middle west is the best place for a writer. It has problems, but it knows it. Midwestern people seem to have more mobility than eastern people, maybe more than southern people.

I get letters every week from people who say, "Grandma Dowdel is from down south! Grandma Dowdel is a Texan, isn't she? I always say, "if you want her to be, yes." Southern traditions probably came up to my part of the state of Illinois.

I think southerners and Midwesterners merge nicely. The fact that we had the war probably makes us think we're more different than we are. But then I explore that in *The River Between Us*, which I think might be my best book. You will see then where my world meets the south.

I am much under the influence of southerners now. I am on the faculty of LSU. I'm adjunct faculty at LSU. Louisiana is the ideal storytelling setting, with its exotic past, glamour, beautiful architecture, and wonderful food. It's the south, but it's its own place, with a different history than the rest of us.

Growing up you were an ardent rule-follower (homework, etc.). Did you ever feel the urge to rebel, even in high school?

Oh, no. I thought rebellion was for people who could afford it. People who didn't have to get good grades because they didn't have to get a scholarship. People who could wreck their car because they could get another one. No, I was more driven by life, and that too made a novelist out of me. Because a novel is always about the consequences of actions.

If you had not become an English teacher or author, what was your other career choice?

It would have to be a career with words. I've wondered now, why as a kid I didn't think, well why not be in journalism? You could live all kinds of places and be a journalist. It never crossed my mind! Now I think it would be a bit of a beginning if all the novelists were newspaper men first, including the novelist Robert Cormier, who I admire the most. He wrote *The Chocolate War*. He came from journalism. They learned about writing to a defined group of people that they knew well and meeting deadlines that cannot be extended. I cannot imagine doing anything that wouldn't have involved language. I am drunk with it.

You have been overheard to say, "You must write by the light of the bridges burning behind you."

I say that because I had to quit my teaching job. I couldn't work part-time and make it work. I was doing homework at night, and grading papers. I had to quit. I had to deny myself an income to sit at the desk and write or die. I just don't see how people can do it part-time. I don't think they can.

You can't produce as much. You can't go out and publicize it for yourself, which you must do because the publishers don't do that.

Did you ever feel you had a low point as an author?

I have low points all the time. I have low points at the beginning of every novel. I don't start with gusto. I write with gathering enthusiasm. I am very low at the beginning of a project. I walk all the way around it a hundred times. I sit at the typewriter all day long and I have a page, and then I throw it out. I am low at the beginning of every novel, which is another reason why I have to throw out the first chapter once I finish the book, and then [re]write the first chapter. It means your first chapter really does anticipate the story. That way, it is written with much more verve and excitement because you're on the downhill! The end is in sight!

From all of your children's books, do you have a favorite character?

There is an elderly character in almost all of them. Because I don't think there are elderly people in the lives of the young now, especially the suburban young, I have to make Grandma Dowdel as a favorite. She changed my whole career. I have a whole new career because of her.

Blossom Culp ignited my early career in the 1970s and has a lot in common with Grandma Dowdel.

You will notice that the renegades in my novels tend to be women, not men. They happen to be girls, not boys. I think it comes from my life. Girls need to explore all of their possibilities. This country gives them wonderful possibilities, and nobody in my novel would regard marriage as a solution. There would be something else.

Blossom Culp and Grandma Dowdel, who are both extreme characters, are probably my most successful.

Is there one letter, or young person you have met, that made a lasting impression?

It's always the last kid that comes up to you, or the last kid you overhear. At this point, they reinforce what I've heard before, but I'm always listening for something new. My best novel, up to *The River Between Us*, and maybe including it, is *Remembering the Good Times*. Somebody wrote and said, "The trouble with your book is that I didn't find it in time." That's the letter that haunts me. I got it twenty years ago.

It's a very sad business, dealing with the young, so as you see I am devoted to humor. They need it. The young aren't generating any. I do believe humor is the best conduit for the message.

You wrote a poem about September 11. From visiting with kids in schools, what is your overall sense of how they view the tragedy?

That it did not happen to them. It is not happening in their history classes. That it was one more thing that happened to adults. Their peer group is their government, and it was not attacked. It horrifies me.

We're at war now, and the young aren't. And they don't know geography. Adolescence is no longer a preparation for adult life. They may never be this powerful again. They live in a much narrower world than I did, being a kid during World War II, learning geography in a very dramatic way. Then knowing that I was going to be drafted in the army made me very aware of the government and what was going on in the world and was there going to be a war when I got into the army. You cannot even imagine it being mandatory to be a soldier, having to serve.

The young are far more provincial than my generation. They almost never look ahead, or at adults, and say, "I'm going to be that. Am I getting ready?"

What responsibilities, in your view, go along with accepting the National Humanities Medal?

By doing anything Mrs. Bush ever asks (he laughs)! She has done something wonderful. She has sent me in October of 2005, as part of the Delegation of American writers, to Madam Putin's Russian Book Festival. I went to Moscow, and I participated in the third annual Russian book festival, which Mrs. Putin patterned upon Mrs. Bush's National Book Festival held in Washington every year. I participated in the first one in 2001, my sister and I, and again in 2004 and 2005.

It was a very high moment in my career to meet Russian teachers and young people. My books are not translated there, and now I wish they were. It is a country waking up after a seventy-year nightmare. It was one of the most exciting places I've ever been. I had never been to Moscow. I would go back tomorrow. It was very exciting. It was fun to be part of that delegation, led by the Librarian of Congress. That's a way my life has changed.

I have been very lucky that my career, shall we say, is coming to its conclusion at the same time the First Lady of the land is a librarian!

You have said that Mark Twain has influenced you. Of your peers, who is your favorite children's author, and why?

Robert Cormier, who is no longer living. He reminded me, in his novel, *The Chocolate War*, of what a book for the young can be now, and what it can do. I think it is the best novel written in the second half of the 20th century. So to have it in our field, he gave me something to look up to. I always need something to look up to. I never had a friend I didn't admire. He's very important to me.

Then, there is this whole faculty of us now, going out around the country, meeting and greeting, and bouncing off each other. Will Hobbs is a good friend of mine because I admire his work. I can admire his work without rivalry. He writes about the great outdoors, and the great west. He's carved out a different territory and I love looking across that. I admire Graham Salisbury's work. There are so many authors I admire. I don't want to leave anyone out. Nobody but a reader ever became a writer. You have to read a thousand books before you can write one. I have to keep reading to keep writing. I have new books around me all the time, and I don't get through them all. Sometimes I say, "I'm not learning anything from this book." But I give it a try.

What inner quality (or personality trait) do you think writers share, since we have such a strong urge to write?

I think we are all failed communicators. If we could have said what we meant the most to the people who meant the most to us, we would not have had to be writers, throwing our messages at strangers. Writers are people standing in the wings of life, trying to make sense of other people's performances, rather than taking center stage.

What are your plans for the future, personal or professional?

I think to the end of the novel, and I say, "Oh, there's another book in that contract." And that's as far as I go. I don't have a hundred novels in my head just waiting to be written down. Some people do. Every time the bucket hits the bottom of the well, as far as I'm concerned! And then in a few weeks I think, wouldn't you feel better if you were writing? Why don't you go to the library and find something to write about. I don't have a five-year plan.

Do you have any regrets?

I'd like to be a better writer than I am. I wish it weren't so hard. But I don't regret it. I know I have to go through what I have to go through to get it on the page. I am so fortunate to have been able to do what I most wanted to do in life, and to make a living at it so that I don't have to do something else. The odds were against it. It happened, so I'm grateful. We're so lucky to be Americans, and to have a wide range of potential readers. And so many stories to tell.

In a past lecture at the University of Illinois/Springfield (2002), you mention you don't have e-mail. Why?

No, not anymore. I used to. I had to get rid of it. I didn't like the way I was acting. I don't want anyone to ever see my rough drafts. And I don't want to see theirs!

Tell me about your latest novel, and other recent news.

The book I am working on in 2006 is a novel of the home front in World War II, which was my grade school years. It is set in a town very much like my old hometown, swollen by war plant production. It is the portrait of my father I hope to get down on paper. The title is *On the Wings of Heroes*.

Chronology

1934   Peck is born on April 5 in Decatur, Illinois.

1935   Peck's mother begins reading to him.

1939   Peck starts kindergarten at Dennis Grade School.

1942   Sister, Cheryl, is born.

1947   In junior high school, he begins to secretly dream of becoming a writer.

1950   Peck, age sixteen, visits New York City for the first time.

1951   He is challenged by his English teacher, Miss Franklin.

1952   Peck is admitted to DePauw University, wanting to become a teacher.

1955   Sails to England on the *Ile de France* to spend his junior year of college at Exeter University.

1956   Peck graduates from college; enlists in the U.S. Army and is stationed in Germany for two years as a chaplain's assistant, sermon writer, and marriage counselor.

1958   Enters graduate school at Southern Illinois University at Carbondale, where he also teaches night school.

1961   English teacher at Glenbrook North High School in Northbrook, Illinois.

1963   Textbook editor for Scott, Foresman and Company in Chicago.

1965   Self-publishes his first book (with Norman Strasma): *Old Town, A Complete Guide: Strolling, Shopping, Supper, Sipping*; moves to New York City to take a job as English teacher at Hunter College and Hunter College High School.

1969   Moves to Washington, D.C. for one year to work for the Council for Basic Education.

1971   Quits teaching job at age thirty-seven to become a writer.

1972   *Don't Look and It Won't Hurt* is published.

1975   *The Ghost Belonged to Me* is published.

1976   *Are You in the House Alone?* is published.

1977   Writes first short story, "Priscilla and the Wimps"; Peck's father dies the day he finishes writing *Father Figure*.

1985   *Remembering the Good Times* is published.

1990   Wins the prestigious Margaret A. Edwards Award.

1995   *The Last Safe Place on Earth* is published.

1999   Wins Newbery Honor for his novel *A Long Way from Chicago*.

2001   Wins the 2001 John Newbery Medal for his novel *A Year Down Yonder*; *Fair Weather* is published.

2002   Is awarded the 2001 National Humanities Medal by President George W. Bush.

2003   *The River Between Us* is published.

2004   Named Member of the Year by the Society of Children's Book Writers and Illustrators; *The Teacher's Funeral* is published.

2005   Travels to Russia to take part in Ludmila
       Putin's Russian Book Festival.

2006   *Here Lies the Librarian* is published.

2007   *On the Wings of Heroes* is published.

Selected Works of Richard Peck

Young Adult Novels

1972	*Don't Look and It Won't Hurt*
1973	*Dreamland Lake*
1973	*Through a Brief Darkness*
1974	*Representing Super Doll*
1975	*The Ghost Belonged to Me*
1976	*Are You in the House Alone?*
1977	*Ghosts I Have Been* (sequel to *The Ghost Belonged to Me*)
1978	*Father Figure*
1979	*Secrets of the Shopping Mall*
1981	*Close Enough to Touch*
1983	*The Dreadful Future of Blossom Culp* (sequel to *Ghosts I Have Been*)
1985	*Remembering the Good Times*
1986	*Blossom Culp and the Sleep of Death*
1987	*Princess Ashley*
1988	*Those Summer Girls I Never Met*
1989	*Voices after Midnight*
1991	*Unfinished Portrait of Jessica*
1993	*Bel-Air Bambi and the Mall Rats*
1995	*The Last Safe Place on Earth*

1995 *Lost in Cyberspace*
1996 *The Great Interactive Dream Machine: Another Adventure in Cyberspace*
1998 *Strays Like Us*
1998 *A Long Way from Chicago: A Novel in Stories*
2000 *A Year Down Yonder*
2001 *Fair Weather*
2003 *The River Between Us*
2004 *The Teacher's Funeral: A Comedy in Three Parts*
2006 *Here Lies the Librarian*
2007 *On the Wings of Heroes*

Picture Books
1977 *Monster Night at Grandma's House* (illustrated by Don Freeman)

Autobiography & Memoir
1991 *Anonymously Yours*
2002 *Invitations to the World: Teaching and Writing for the Young*

Adult Novels
1980 *Amanda/Miranda*
1981 *New York Time*
1983 *This Family of Women*
1998 *London Holiday*

Short Story Anthologies
2004 *Past Perfect, Present Tense: New and Collected Short Stories*

CHAPTER
NOTES

Chapter 1. Burning Bridges

1. Candi Moonshower, "Epiphanies in Los Angeles: What I Learned From SCBWI Conferences," *Borderlines*, no. 55, 2005, p. 4.

2. Richard Peck, *Don't Look and It Won't Hurt* (New York: Henry Holt, 1972), p. 9.

3. Richard Peck, *Noted Children's Author*, The Illinois Channel, 2002, DVD.

4. Donald Gallo, *Presenting Richard Peck* (Boston: Twayne, 1989), p. 20.

5. Richard Peck, *Invitations to the World* (New York: Dial, 2002), pp. 34–36.

6. Ibid., p. 37.

7. Gallo, p. 7.

8. Peck, *Invitations to the World*, pp. 26–27.

9. "Richard Peck," *Something About the Author Autobiography Series*, vol. 2:178.

10. Gallo, p. 7.

11. "Richard Peck Papers," De Grummond Children's Literature Collection, July 2001, <http://www.lib.usm.edu/~degrum/html/research/findaids/peck.htm#bio> (August 28, 2006).

12. Peck, *Invitations to the World*, p. 54.

13. Interview by Scholastic Students, "Richard Peck's Interview Transcript," n.d., <http://books. scholastic.com/teachers/authorsandbooks/ authorstudies/authorhome.jsp?authorID=5557& displayName=Interview%20Transcript> (August 28, 2006).

Chapter 2. Farming the Folks

1. Richard Peck, *Invitations to the World* (New York: Dial Books, 2002), p. 10.
2. Richard Peck, "A Note From Richard Peck," Dial Books Flyer/Brochure (New York, March 2003), p. 2.
3. Peck, *Invitations to the World*, pp. 10–11.
4. Richard Peck, *Noted Children's Author*, The Illinois Channel, 2002, DVD.
5. Donald Gallo, *Presenting Richard Peck* (Boston: Twayne, 1989), p. 8.
6. "Richard Peck," *Authors and Artists for Young Adults*, vols. 7–26, Gale Research, 1992–1999.
7. Gallo, pp. 7–8.
8. Author interview with Richard Peck, January 19, 2006.
9. Gallo, pp. 6–7.
10. Peck, *Invitations to the World*, p. 83.
11. Richard Peck, *Noted Children's Author*, The Illinois Channel, 2002, lecture on DVD.
12. Richard Peck, *Monster Night at Grandma's House* (New York: Viking, 1977), p. 8.
13. Gallo, pp. 9–10.
14. Gallo, p. 9.
15. Author interview with Richard Peck, January 19, 2006.
16. *Something About the Author Autobiography Series*, p. 181.

17. Richard Peck, *Anonymously Yours* (New York: Simon & Schuster, 1991), pp. 7 and 57.
18. Author interview with Richard Peck, January 19, 2006.
19. Richard Peck, *Anonymously Yours*, p. 1.

Chapter 3. University Days—and Wartime

1. Richard Peck, *Anonymously Yours* (New York: Simon & Schuster, 1991), p. 70.
2. Ibid., pp. 2–3.
3. Ibid.
4. Ibid., pp. 4–6.
5. DePauw University News (no author noted), "Author Richard Peck '56 a 'Master of Nostalgia for a Simpler Past,' Writes *Houston Chronicle*," February 4, 2005, <http://www.depauw.edu/news/index.asp?id=15319> (September 4, 2006).
6. Peck, *Anonymously Yours*, pp. 74–78.
7. Donald Gallo, *Presenting Richard Peck* (Boston: Twayne, 1989), p. 12.
8. Peck, *Anonymously Yours*, p. 78.

Chapter 4. The English Teacher

1. Richard Peck, *Anonymously Yours* (New York: Simon & Schuster, 1991), p. 82.
2. Ibid., p. 81.
3. Ibid., p. 84.
4. Donald Gallo, *Presenting Richard Peck* (Boston: Twayne, 1989), p. 14.
5. *Are You in the House Alone?* 1978 television movie by CBS-TV.
6. Peck, *Anonymously Yours*, p. 85.

7. Lynn Fabian Lasner, "Making a Difference: The National Humanities Medalists: Richard Peck: Writing for the Next Generation," *Humanities: The Magazine of the National Endowment for the Humanities*, vol. 23, no. 3, May/June 2002, <http://www.neh.gov/news/humanities/2002-05/medalists.html#peck> (September 4, 2006).

8. Richard Peck, *Invitations to the World* (New York: Dial, 2002), pp. 71–72.

Chapter 5. A Higher Calling

1. Richard Peck, *Invitations to the World* (New York: Dial, 2002), p. 62.

2. Richard Peck, *Anonymously Yours* (New York: Simon & Schuster, 1991), p. 92.

3. Donald Gallo, *Presenting Richard Peck* (Boston: Twayne, 1989), p. 15.

4. Peck, *Anonymously Yours*, pp. 93–94.

5. "1960s," *Wikipedia*, October 2006, <http://en.wikipedia.org/wiki/1960s> (September 4, 2006).

6. Peck, *Anonymously Yours*, p. 94.

7. Richard Peck, "Books for the Readers of the 21st Century," The Ezra Jack Keats Lecture, March 24, 2000. <http://www.lib.usm.edu/~degrum/html/aboutus/au-fall2000keatslecture.shtml> (November 2, 2006).

8. Gallo, p. 57.

9. Peck, "Books for the Readers of the 21st Century."

10. Richard Peck, "A Note From Richard Peck," Dial Books Flyer/Brochure (New York, March 2003), p. 2.

11. "Richard Peck," *Authors and Artists for Young Adults*, vols. 7–26, Gale Research, 1992–1999. Reproduced in *Biography Resource Center*, Farmington Hills, Mich.: Thomson Gale, 2006, <http://galenet.galegroup.com.proxy.library. emory.edu/servlet/BioRC> (September 4, 2006).

Chapter 6. Writing for Generation "Next"

1. Richard Peck, *Anonymously Yours* (New York: Simon & Schuster, 1991), p. 97.
2. Ibid., pp. 100–101.
3. Ibid., p. 104.
4. Ibid., p. 105.
5. Richard Peck, *Invitations to the World* (New York: Dial, 2002), p. 169.
6. Richard Peck, *Fair Weather: A Conversation with Richard Peck*, Fall 2002, (New York: Penguin Putnam), p. 146.

Chapter 7. The Newberys and the White House

1. Richard Peck, Newbery Medal acceptance speech, *The Horn Book Magazine*, July 1, 2001, vol. 77, no. 4, p. 398.
2. Ibid.
3. Review of *A Long Way from Chicago. Publishers Weekly*, July 6, 1998, *Barnes & Noble.com*, 1997–2006, <http://search.barnesandnoble. com/booksearch/isbninquiry.asp? ean= 9780141303529&z=y> (November 2, 2006).
4. Richard Peck, "Commentary by Richard Peck," Penguin Web site, n.d., <http://us.penguingroup. com/static/rguides/us/richard_peck.html> (September 7, 2006).
5. Ibid.

6. Mike Frazier, "Cerro Gordo Celebrates 150th Birthday," *Herald & Review* newspaper, Decatur, Illinois, June 18, 2005, <http://www.herald-review.com/articles/2005/06/19/news/local_news/1008555.txt> (September 7, 2006).

7. Author interview with Richard Peck, January 19, 2006.

8. Richard Peck, *A Year Down Yonder* (New York: Dial, 2000), pp. 26–27.

9. Johnson and Giorgis, p. 392.

10. Richard Peck, Newbery Medal acceptance speech, p. 401.

11. Richard Peck, *Invitations to the World* (New York: Dial, 2002), pp. 191–192.

12. Ibid., p. 193.

13. Office of the Press Secretary, Whitehouse.gov, "President, Mrs. Bush Present Arts & Humanities Medals—Remarks by the President and Mrs. Bush at Presentation of the 2001 National Medal of Arts and National Humanities Medal Awards," Washington D.C., <http://www.whitehouse.gov/news/releases/2002/04/20020422-3.html#> (September 7, 2006).

14. (author unknown) "Adjunct Professor Richard Peck Receives National Humanities Medal," LSU Highlights, vol. 30, Spring 2002, <http://www.lsu.edu/highlights/023/ hmedal.htm> (September 7, 2006).

Chapter 8. A Literary Maverick

1. Richard Peck, *Past Perfect, Present Tense: New and Collected Short Stories* (New York: Dial, 2004), pp. 4–7.

2. Ibid., p. 8.

3. Compiled by Elizabeth Koehler-Pentacoff, *The ABC's of Writing for Children* (Sanger, Calif.: Quill Driver Books, 2003), pp. 62–63.

4. Richard Peck, "Battered by Left and by Right: Censorship in the '90s as Viewed by a Novelist From Illinois Whose Books Have Wound Up on Forbidden Lists," Illinois Issues, July 1993, <http://www.lib.niu.edu/ipo/1993/ii930724.html> (September 7, 2006).

5. "Teacher's Guide: *The Last Safe Place on Earth*," Teachers@Random Web site, Random House Children's Books, <http://www.randomhouse.com/teachers/catalog/display.pperl? isbn= 9780440220077&view=tg>.

6. Richard Peck, "Books for the Readers of the 21st Century," The Ezra Jack Keats Lecture, March 24, 2000, <http://www.lib.usm.edu/~degrum/html/aboutus/au-fall2000keatslecture.shtml> (November 2, 2006).

7. Richard Peck, *Fair Weather: A Conversation with Richard Peck* (New York: Penguin Putnam, 2002), p. 142.

8. Nancy J. Johnson and Cyndi Giorgis, "2001 Newbery Medal winner: A Conversation with Richard Peck," *The Reading Teacher*, vol. 55, no. 4, December 2001/January 2002, pp. 393–394.

9. (author not noted), "Adjunct Professor Richard Peck Receives National Humanities Medal," LSU Highlights, vol. 30, Spring 2002, <http://www.lsu.edu/highlights/023/hmedal.htm> (September 7, 2006).

10. Author interview with Richard Peck, January 19, 2006.

Richard Peck

Chapter 9. A Teacher at Heart

1. Richard Peck, *Embracing the Child Pa*ge, n.d., <http://www.embracingthechild.org/apeck.html> (September 9, 2006).

2. Richard Peck, *Invitations to the World* (New York: Dial Books, 2002), pp. 13–14.

3. Ibid., pp. 198–199.

4. Richard Peck, "Books for the Readers of the 21st Century," The Ezra Jack Keats Lecture, March 24, 2000, <http://www.lib.usm.edu/~degrum/html/aboutus/au-fall2000keatslecture.shtml> (September 10, 2006).

5. "Richard Peck," *Authors and Artists for Young Adults*, vols. 7–26, Gale Research, 1992–1999, <http://galenet.galegroup.com.proxy.library. emory.edu/servlet/BioRC> (September 10, 2006).

6. "Bulletin: News and Notes," Society of Children's Book Writers & Illustrators, Los Angeles, September/October 2004, p. 3. <http://www.scbwi.org/pubs/bulletin/sept_oct_04/news_notes.htm>.

7. Nancy J. Johnson and Cyndi Giorgis, "2001 Newbery Medal Winner: A Conversation with Richard Peck," *Reading Teacher*, vol. 55, no. 4, December 2001/January 2002, p. 395.

8. Callie Clark, "Author Making Return to Scene of Stories," *Southeast Missourian*, January 15, 2005, <http://www.semissourian.com/story.html$rec=154375> (September 10, 2006).

9. Ernest Hemingway, "Mark Twain," Wikipedia, n.d., <http://en.wikipedia.org/wiki/Mark_Twain> (September 10, 2006).

10. Author interview with Lauri Hornik (Peck's editor at Penguin Putnam/Dial Books), February 2, 2006.

11. Richard Peck, "2004 National Book Festival—Richard Peck," October 9, 2004, <http://www.researchchannel.org/program/displayevent.asp?rid=2601> (September 10, 2006).

12. Ibid.

13. Richard Peck, "A Note from Richard Peck," Dial Books Flyer/Brochure (New York, March 2003), p. 2.

14. Peck, *Invitations to the World*, p. 195.

15. Catherine Gourley, "Richard Peck: Researching Fiction," *Writing*, Stamford, November/December 2001, p. 26.

Glossary

anthology—A collection of selected literary pieces (such as stories or poems).

basic training—Also known as boot camp, it is the initial military training for Army, Navy, Air Force, and Marine recruits where they are "drilled": to stand, march, and respond to orders in an unquestioning manner.

bomb shelter—Structure for the protection of people (civilians or military) against enemy attacks from the air.

book banning—The practice of forbidding access to a controversial book. (*See also* censorship.)

Brothers Grimm—German authors of the early nineteenth century, Jacob Ludwig Carl Grimm and Wilhelm Carl Grimm, who cowrote *Grimm's Fairy Tales*, which included "Hansel and Gretel," "Little Red Riding Hood," "Rumpelstiltskin," "Snow White and the Seven Dwarfs," and others.

censorship—The practice of examining in order to suppress or delete anything considered objectionable.

civil rights—The rights of personal liberty guaranteed to all U.S. citizens by the 13th and 14th Amendments to the Constitution and by acts of Congress.

3333

3333

Daughters of the American Revolution—Founded in 1890, DAR is a volunteer women's service organization dedicated to promoting patriotism, preserving American history, and securing America's future through better education for children. Also, members must have an ancestor who fought in the Revolution.

draft board—Government unit that would classify registrants (usually males, who had reached the age of eighteen) to determine whether they were to serve in the armed forces.

dysfunctional relationship—A relationship in which two people make an emotional "contract" and agree to meet each other's needs in what ends up being self-destructive ways.

epiphany—A revealing scene or moment.

Farmer's Almanac—Published since 1818, it is a book that includes astronomical tables, weather forecasts for the regions of the United States, and helpful tidbits (some factual and some considered suspicious).

Flexible Flyer—A sled.

fraternity—A men's student organization formed chiefly for social purposes that has secret rites and a name consisting of Greek letters.

generation gap—A difference in values and attitudes, especially between young people and their parents or grandparents.

Halliburton, Richard—American author, daredevil, and adventurer born in 1900 and who died in 1939.

honorary degree—An extraordinary academic degree awarded to an individual for his or her valuable contribution to society.

livable wage—Income sufficient to meet a family's basic needs (food, housing, child care, transportation, health care, clothing, household and personal expenses, insurance, and retirement savings).

mantra—A slogan or motto.

Midwest—Land region of the United States usually defined by the following states: Illinois, Indiana, Iowa, Kansas, Michigan, Minnesota, Missouri, Nebraska, North Dakota, Ohio, South Dakota, and Wisconsin.

Model A Ford—Ford Motor Company automobile that was introduced in 1927.

National Honor Society—An organization of middle and high school students, whose members must show achievement in the areas of scholarship, leadership, service, and character.

point of view—A position from which something is considered or evaluated.

privy—An old-fashioned term for an outdoor toilet (outhouse).

problem novels—Fiction dealing with topics such as divorce, death, suicide, rape, and pregnancy.

rural—An area of farms or countryside such as small towns and villages. Populations are smaller in these areas.

terrorist—A person who violently attacks people and places in hopes of political or social gain.

tongue-in-cheek—A style of humor in which things are said only half seriously, or in a subtly mocking, exaggerated, or ironic way.

tour of duty—In the military, it is a period of time spent at sea or assigned to service in a foreign country.

Twain, Mark—Pen name of Samuel Langhorne Clemens (1835–1910), a humorous and witty Midwest American author.

Uncle Sam—A personification of the United States Army, whose face appeared on various wartime media and posters.

Victorian Era—Characteristics of the reign of Queen Victoria of England (1837–1901), a time of proper and sometimes strict moral behavior.

Vietnam War (1957–1975)—A conflict in which North Vietnam fought against South Vietnam (and its allies) to unify the country under communist rule.

FURTHER READING

Books

Collier, Laurie, and Joyce Nakamura, eds. *Major Authors and Illustrators for Children and Young Adults*. NY: Thomson Gale, 1993.

Gallo, Donald R. *Presenting Richard Peck*. New York: Dell, 1993.

Peck, Richard. *Anonymously Yours*. New York: Simon & Schuster, 1991.

Sommers, Michael A. *Richard Peck*. New York: Rosen, 2003.

Internet Addresses

Richard Peck, Featured Author
http://www.carolhurst.com/authors/rpeck.html

Educational Paperback Association: Richard Peck
http://www.edupaperback.org/showauth.cfm?authid=68

Library of Congress National Book Festival: Richard Peck
http://www.loc.gov/bookfest/authors/peck.html

Index